R & J & Z

By Melody Bates

DRAMATIS PERSONAE

ROMEO MONTAGUE
A young nobleman of Verona, in love with and recently married to Juliet.

BALTHASAR
A young man of Verona, friends with and employed by Romeo.

THE APOTHECARY
Former student of Friar Lawrence: an evil mastermind. Has a shop in Mantua.

FRIAR LAWRENCE
A priest in Verona, chief confidant of Romeo & Juliet. Highly versed in naturally-derived medicines, drugs, and occult lore.

FRIAR JOHN
A priest, of Friar Lawrence's order.

PARIS
A nobleman of Verona; engaged to Juliet.

PARIS' PAGE
A young page, easily frightened.

JULIET CAPULET
A young noblewoman of Verona, in love with and recently married to Romeo.

FIRST SEARCHER
A female Veronese official charged with examining all dead bodies to determine whether or not they died of the plague. Also part of a secret, ancient order with a deeper purpose. A formidable fighter, not entirely trustworthy.

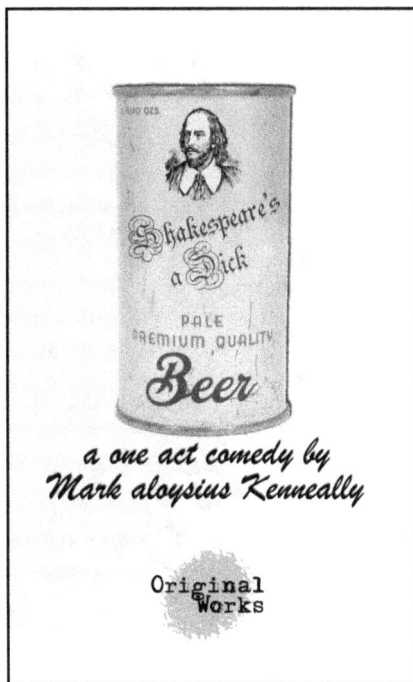

a one act comedy by
Mark aloysius Kenneally

Original Works

Shakespeare's a Dick
by Mark aloysius Kenneally

Synopsis: When the young redneck Wally curses the name of Shakespeare and opts to attend a Monster Truck Show instead of "As You Like It," he feels the wrath of the Bard. Waking up after a heavy night of boozing, he finds he can only speak in Shakespearian verse. His best friend Ramie searches for a cure from their high school English teacher Ingrid, while his girlfriend Doris swoons for the new Wally.

Cast Size: 2 Males, 2 Females

SECOND SEARCHER
The First Searcher's partner in official and secret duties. Also a formidable fighter. The more trustworthy of the two women.

PRINCE ESCALUS
Prince of Verona. Dies early.

LADY CAPULET
Juliet's mother.

LORD CAPULET
Juliet's father.

LORD MONTAGUE
Romeo's father.

TYBALT
Juliet's cousin. Deceased at the start of the play.

MERCUTIO
Romeo's best friend. A wild child—the life of the party. Deceased at the start of the play.

A BOY
An orphan in service to the Apothecary.

ROSALINE
Former crush of Romeo's.

THE HORDE
A horde of undead revenants in thrall to the Apothecary. Includes Juliet's Nurse.

TIME and PLACE: R & J & Z begins very late on a Thursday night in mid-July, at the end of the 16th Century. The events play out over the course of the following day and night in Verona and Mantua, Italy.

R & J & Z was developed in partnership with Opera House Arts in Stonington, ME, where it had its world premiere in July 2014, directed by Joan Jubett.

CAST

ROMEO: Matt Hurley
JULIET: Melody Bates
MERCUTIO: J.Stephen Brantley
FRIAR LAWRENCE: Peter Richards
TYBALT: Per Janson
FIRST SEARCHER: Yvonne Roen
SECOND SEARCHER: Cait Cortelyou
APOTHECARY: Rachel Murdy
BALTHAZAR: D. T. Bennett
PAGE: Marvin Merritt IV
ESCALUS: Rachel Murdy
PARIS: J.Stephen Brantley
LADY CAPULET: Cherie Mason
CAPULET: Jeff Brink
MONTAGUE: Larry Estey
BOY: Ian Cust
FRIAR JOHN: Elena Kirk
ROSALINE: Nicole Nolan
ENSEMBLE/ HORDE: Maude Burke, Callie Jacks, Emma Grace Keenan

R & J & Z had its New York premiere in April 2015 at the New Ohio Theatre, produced by Hard Sparks and directed by Joan Jubett. 2015 New York Innovative Theatre Awards Nominations: Outstanding Revival of a Play, Lighting Design, Winner for Innovative Design (Gore and Special Effects)

CAST

ROMEO: Matt Hurley
JULIET: Melody Bates
MERCUTIO: J.Stephen Brantley
FRIAR LAWRENCE: Warren Jackson
TYBALT: Per Janson
FIRST SEARCHER: Margi Douglas
SECOND SEARCHER: Cait Cortelyou
APOTHECARY: Rachel Murdy
BALTHAZAR: David Bennett
PAGE: Marshall Spann
ESCALUS: Drae Campbell
PARIS: Blaze Mancillas
LADY CAPULET: Elizabeth Bell
CAPULET: Randy Howk
MONTAGUE: Chris Tramantana
BOY: Clara Sanchez-Vela / August Geraci
FRIAR JOHN: Russell Sperberg
ROSALINE: Michele Quintero
NURSE: Drae Campbell

R & J & Z

ACT I, SCENE 1
Mantua: A street in front of the Apothecary's shop

[Deep night, just before dawn. ROMEO is sleeping on the ground, passed out in front of the APOTHECARY OF MANTUA's evil-looking shop. At first we are not sure that ROMEO is alive. Something is not right about the way his body lies there. Then, he stirs. He is dreaming. We watch this. It is unsettling. He could be having a very bad dream or a very good dream. Suddenly, he wakes.]

ROMEO
I dreamt my lady came and found me dead—
Strange dream, that gives a dead man leave to think!—
And breathed such life with kisses in my lips,
That I revived, and was an emperor.
Ah me! how sweet is love itself possessed,
When but love's shadows are so rich in joy!

[Enter BALTHASAR]

News from Verona!—How now, Balthasar!
Dost thou not bring me letters from the friar?
How doth my lady? Is my father well?
How fares my Juliet? that I ask again;
For nothing can be ill, if she be well.

BALTHASAR
Then she is well, and nothing can be ill:
Her body sleeps in Capel's monument,
And her immortal part with angels lives.

I saw her laid low in her kindred's vault,
And presently took post to tell it you:
O, pardon me for bringing these ill news,
Since you did leave it for my office, sir.

ROMEO
Is it even so? then I defy you, stars!
Thou know'st my lodging: get me ink and paper,
And hire post-horses; I will hence tonight.

BALTHASAR
I do beseech you, sir, have patience:
Your looks are pale and wild, and do import
Some misadventure.

ROMEO
                              Tush, thou art deceived:
Leave me, and do the thing I bid thee do.
Hast thou no letters to me from the friar?

BALTHASAR
No, my good lord.

ROMEO
                              No matter: get thee gone,
And hire those horses; I'll be with thee straight.

[BALTHASAR exits]

Well, Juliet, I will lie with thee tonight.
Let's see for means: O mischief, thou art swift
To enter in the thoughts of desperate men!
I do remember an apothecary,—

And hereabouts he dwells,—which late I noted
In tattered weeds, with overwhelming brows,
Culling of simples; meagre were his looks,
Sharp misery had worn him to the bones:
And in his needy shop a tortoise hung,
An alligator stuffed, and other skins
Of ill-shaped fishes; and about his shelves
A beggarly account of empty boxes,
Green earthen pots, bladders and musty seeds,
Remnants of packthread and old cakes of roses,
Were thinly scattered, to make up a show.
Noting this penury, to myself I said
'An if a man did need a poison now,
Whose sale is present death in Mantua,
Here lives a caitiff wretch would sell it him.'
O, this same thought did but forerun my need;
And this same needy man must sell it me.
As I remember, this should be the house.
Being holiday, the beggar's shop is shut.
What, ho! apothecary!

*[He bangs on the door. The APOTHECARY opens it,
disheveled.]*

APOTHECARY
Who calls so loud?

ROMEO
Come hither, man. I see that thou art poor:
Hold, there is forty ducats: let me have
A dram of poison, such soon-speeding gear
As will disperse itself through all the veins
That the life-weary taker may fall dead

And that the trunk may be discharged of breath
As violently as hasty powder fired
Doth hurry from the fatal cannon's womb.

APOTHECARY
Such mortal drugs I have; but Mantua's law
Is death to any he that utters them.

ROMEO
Art thou so bare and full of wretchedness,
And fear'st to die? famine is in thy cheeks,
Need and oppression starveth in thine eyes,
Contempt and beggary hangs upon thy back;
The world is not thy friend nor the world's law;
The world affords no law to make thee rich;
Then be not poor, but break it, and take this.

APOTHECARY
My poverty, but not my will, consents.

ROMEO
I pay thy poverty, and not thy will.

APOTHECARY
Put this in any liquid thing you will,
And drink it off; and, if you had the strength
Of twenty men, it would dispatch you straight.

ROMEO
There is thy gold, worse poison to men's souls,
Doing more murders in this loathsome world,
Than these poor compounds that thou mayst not sell.
I sell thee poison; thou hast sold me none.

Farewell: buy food, and get thyself in flesh.
Come, cordial and not poison, go with me
To Juliet's grave; for there must I use thee.
[Exeunt]

ACT I, SCENE 2
Verona: The Graveyard

*[Enter the SEARCHERS of the Town, cloaked. They move
stealthily through the churchyard, prodding new graves,
scanning the periphery.]*

SECOND SEARCHER
There's three fresh graves dug up and robbed tonight.

FIRST SEARCHER
The corpses gone, or just the valuables?

SECOND SEARCHER
The corpses. Who is taking them? And how
Have we not seen the thief, patrolling here
Amidst the graves as we do every night?

FIRST SEARCHER
Perhaps you fell asleep while on your watch.

SECOND SEARCHER
I never slept, sister. My oath is sacred.
Your mood is sour tonight.

FIRST SEARCHER
                                        Or perhaps you
Were off deflow'ring stablehands again.
You really ought to let the poor boys be—

SECOND SEARCHER
My unofficial hours are mine own.
Freedom is for using, sister, you know that:

Those lucky boys are none the worse for me.
You ought to try it—a bit of slackening
Might do you good.

FIRST SEARCHER

                        If slackness were my goal,
It would not have loose hay straws in its hair.
You aim low, sister. I'd not stoop so low.

SECOND SEARCHER
Well, as you will. *[a new thought]* That priest, two nights
ago—
You let him go?

FIRST SEARCHER
                        There was no plague. I kept
Him locked up till tonight. These priests. Such busy
Bodies.

SECOND SEARCHER
        Hold—there is a track here—as of
A body dragged. This is some new mischief.
You're certain you saw nothing on your watch?

FIRST SEARCHER
Nothing. *[a beat. She changes the subject.]*
        Sister, do you ever long
For something more than what our lives are now?

SECOND SEARCHER
What, a husband?

FIRST SEARCHER
                        No. Not less power: more.

SECOND SEARCHER
There is great honor in the work we do—
And danger, which takes fortitude to face.
Our training makes us strong, our calling keeps
Us free: for me, that power is enough.

FIRST SEARCHER
Some nights it is not quite enough for me.

SECOND SEARCHER
But there's an older purpose to our order:
Ancienter evils we are sworn to watch for.
By day we seek out plague; report on it—
By night we search for something far more grim.
The annals of our Sisterhood contain
A list of harbingers that presage dire
Catastrophe—the rising of the dead;
And ever vigilant, we stand the watch,
That when or if the bloody tide should come,
The Searchers will defend the world against it.

FIRST SEARCHER
You are a dreamer, sister. Airy notions
Of dead come back to life for us to fight
May well beguile a story-telling hour,
But that is all they are. We do our work.

SECOND SEARCHER
I think the time is near. The signs abound:
The opening of graves; the heaps of dead;
The creeping sickness in the populace—
These omens stand in writing in our books.

FIRST SEARCHER
The mothy fantasies of moldering texts.

SECOND SEARCHER
But what of Mantua eight months ago?
We fought a creature who had surely died.

FIRST SEARCHER
He was dying of the ordinary plague,
And nothing more exotic was at play.

FRIAR JOHN *[off]*
Holy Franciscan friar! brother, ho!

FIRST SEARCHER
Hoods up, sister. We should not be seen.
If any apprehend thee, say thou art
The night's watch.

SECOND SEARCHER
                                Unless the dead should rise tonight,
And we are called upon to fight them off,
Revealing our true purpose to the world—

FRIAR JOHN *[entering]*
Friar Lawrence!

*[The FIRST SEARCHER hushes the SECOND
SEARCHER, motioning for her to take cover. They vanish
into the dark as FRIAR LAWRENCE enters, meeting
FRIAR JOHN.]*

FRIAR LAWRENCE
Friar John!
Welcome from Mantua: what says Romeo?
Or, if his mind be writ, give me his letter.

FRIAR JOHN
The searchers of the town,
Suspecting that I had been in a house
Where the infectious pestilence did reign,
Sealed up the doors, and would not let me forth;
So that my speed to Mantua there was stayed.

FRIAR LAWRENCE
Who bare my letter, then, to Romeo?

FRIAR JOHN
I could not send it,—here it is again,—
Nor get a messenger to bring it thee,
So fearful were they of infection.

FRIAR LAWRENCE
Unhappy fortune! by my brotherhood,
The letter was not nice but full of charge
Of dear import, and the neglecting it
May do much danger.
Now must I to the monument alone;
Within three hours will fair Juliet wake:
Poor living corse, closed in a dead man's tomb!

[From off, we hear PARIS calling to his PAGE.]

PARIS
Give me thy torch, boy:

[The priests hurry out of sight as PARIS and his PAGE enter.]
                              hence, and stand aloof:
Yet put it out, for I would not be seen.
Hold thou thine ear close to the hollow ground;
So shall no foot upon the churchyard tread,
Being loose, unfirm, with digging up of graves,
But thou shalt hear it: whistle then to me,
As signal that thou hear'st something approach.
Give me those flowers. Do as I bid thee, go.

PAGE
[Aside] I am almost afraid to stand alone
Here in the churchyard; yet I will adventure.
[He retreats back among the tombs.]

PARIS
Sweet flower, with flowers thy bridal bed I strew,--
O woe! thy canopy is dust and stones;--
Which with sweet water nightly I will dew—
[The Page whistles.]
The boy gives warning something doth approach.
[Enter ROMEO and BALTHASAR. PARIS hides.]

ROMEO
Give me that mattock and the wrenching iron.
Hold, take this letter; early in the morning
See thou deliver it to my lord and father.
Give me the light: upon thy life, I charge thee,
Whate'er thou hear'st or seest, stand all aloof,
And do not interrupt me in my course.
But if thou, jealous, dost return to pry
In what I further shall intend to do,

By heaven, I will tear thee joint by joint
And strew this hungry churchyard with thy limbs!

BALTHASAR
I will be gone, sir, and not trouble you.

ROMEO
So shalt thou show me friendship. Take thou that:
Live, and be prosperous: and farewell, good fellow.

BALTHASAR
[Aside] For all this same, I'll hide me hereabout:
His looks I fear, and his intents I doubt.
[He hides.]

ROMEO
Thou detestable maw, thou womb of death,
Gorged with the dearest morsel of the earth,
Thus I enforce thy rotten jaws to open,
And, in despite, I'll cram thee with more food!
[He opens the tomb.]

PARIS *[Coming forward]*
Stop thy unhallowed toil, vile Montague!
Condemned villain, I do apprehend thee:
Obey, and go with me; for thou must die.

ROMEO
I must indeed; and therefore came I hither.
Good gentle youth, tempt not a desperate man;
Fly hence, and leave me: think upon these gone;
Let them affright thee. I beseech thee, youth!

PARIS
I do defy thy conjurations,
And apprehend thee for a felon here.

ROMEO
Wilt thou provoke me? then have at thee, boy!
[They fight.]

PAGE
O Lord, they fight! I will go call the watch.

PARIS
O, I am slain! If thou be merciful,
Open the tomb, lay me with Juliet.
[He dies.]

ROMEO
In faith, I will. Let me peruse this face.
Mercutio's kinsman, noble County Paris!
I'll bury thee in a triumphant grave;
A grave? O no! a lantern, slaughtered youth,
For here lies Juliet, and her beauty makes
This vault a feasting presence full of light.
O my love! my wife!
Death, that hath sucked the honey of thy breath,
Hath had no power yet upon thy beauty:
Thou art not conquered; beauty's ensign yet
Is crimson in thy lips and in thy cheeks,
And death's pale flag is not advanced there.
Tybalt, liest thou there in thy bloody sheet?
O, what more favor can I do to thee,
Than with that hand that cut thy youth in twain
To sunder his that was thine enemy?

Forgive me, cousin! Ah, dear Juliet,
Why art thou yet so fair? shall I believe
That unsubstantial death is amorous,
And that the lean abhorred monster keeps
Thee here in dark to be his paramour?
For fear of that, I still will stay with thee;
And never from this palace of dim night
Depart again: here, here will I remain
With worms that are thy chamber-maids; O, here
Will I set up my everlasting rest,
And shake the yoke of inauspicious stars
From this world-wearied flesh. Eyes, look your last!
Arms, take your last embrace! and, lips, O you
The doors of breath, seal with a righteous kiss
A dateless bargain to engrossing death!
Come, bitter conduct, come, unsavory guide!
Thou desperate pilot, now at once run on
The dashing rocks thy sea-sick weary bark!
Here's to my love!
[Drinks]
O true apothecary!
Thy drugs are quick. Thus with a kiss I die.
[He contorts and dies. The drug is quick, but not
pleasant. Enter FRIAR LAWRENCE, with a lantern,
crowbar, and shovel. Balthasar reappears.]

FRIAR LAWRENCE
Who's there?

BALTHASAR
          A friend, and one that knows you well.

FRIAR LAWRENCE
Bliss be upon you! Tell me, good my friend,
What torch is yond, that vainly lends his light
To grubs and eyeless skulls? as I discern,
It burneth in the Capel's monument.

BALTHASAR
It doth so, holy sir; and there's my master,
One that you love.

FRIAR LAWRENCE
                    Who is it?

BALTHASAR
                              Romeo.

FRIAR LAWRENCE
Romeo!
Alack, alack, what blood is this, which stains
The stony entrance of this sepulchre?
*[He enters the tomb and immediately sees signs of terrible
danger. He examines Romeo's body, checking his eyelids
and recoiling at what he sees.]*
Romeo! O, pale! Who else? what, Paris too?
And steeped in blood? The lady stirs.
[JULIET wakes]

JULIET
O comfortable friar! where is my lord?
I do remember well where I should be,
And there I am. Where is my Romeo?
[A frightening noise]

FRIAR LAWRENCE
Lady, come from that nest
Of death, contagion, and unnatural sleep:
A greater power than we can contradict
Hath thwarted our intents. Come, come away.
Thy husband in thy bosom there lies dead;
And Paris too. Come, go, good Juliet,
[The noise, again]
I dare no longer stay.

JULIET
Go, get thee hence, for I will not away.
[FRIAR LAWRENCE runs out of the tomb and exits.]
What's here? a cup, closed in my true love's hand?
Poison, I see, hath been his timeless end:
O churl! drunk all, and left no friendly drop
To help me after? I will kiss thy lips;
Haply some poison yet doth hang on them,
To make me die with a restorative.
[She kisses him, sucking the poison from his lips]
Thy lips are warm.

FIRST SEARCHER [AS NIGHT'S WATCH]
[Within]   Lead, boy: which way?

JULIET
Yea, noise? then I'll be brief. O happy dagger!
[She snatches ROMEO's dagger.]

This is thy sheath; there rust, and let me die.

*[She stabs herself. She bleeds in gushes all over
everything. Stumbling, stabbing, her blood gets all over*

the other bodies—Tybalt, Paris, Romeo are all covered in
her blood. She falls on ROMEO's body and dies. The
FIRST SEARCHER, hooded, enters with the PAGE of
Paris.]

PAGE
This is the place; there, where the torch doth burn.

FIRST SEARCHER [AS NIGHT'S WATCH]
The ground is bloody; search about the churchyard:
Pitiful sight! here lies the county slain,
And Juliet bleeding, warm, and newly dead,
Who here hath lain these two days buried.
Go, tell the prince: run to the Capulets:
Raise up the Montagues:

[The PAGE runs out calling for help. The SECOND
SEARCHER, hooded, enters with BALTHASAR and
FRIAR LAWRENCE.]

SECOND SEARCHER [AS NIGHT'S WATCH]
Here's Romeo's man; I found him in the churchyard.

FIRST SEARCHER [AS NIGHT'S WATCH]
Hold him in safety, till the prince come hither.

SECOND SEARCHER [AS NIGHT'S WATCH]
Here is a friar, that trembles, sighs and weeps:
I took this mattock and this spade from him,
As he was coming from this churchyard side.

FIRST SEARCHER [AS NIGHT'S WATCH]
A great suspicion: stay the friar too.

*[PRINCE ESCALUS enters, followed by LORD and LADY
CAPULET and the PAGE.]*

PRINCE
What misadventure is so early up,
That calls our person from our morning's rest?

CAPULET
What should it be, that they so shriek abroad?

LADY CAPULET
The people in the street cry Romeo,
Some Juliet, and some Paris; and all run,
With open outcry toward our monument.

PRINCE
What fear is this which startles in our ears?

FIRST SEARCHER [AS NIGHT'S WATCH]
Sovereign, here lies the County Paris slain;
And Romeo dead; and Juliet, dead before,
Warm and new killed.

SECOND SEARCHER [AS NIGHT'S WATCH]
Here is a friar, and slaughtered Romeo's man;
With instruments upon them, fit to open
These dead men's tombs.

CAPULET
O heavens! O wife, look how our daughter bleeds!

LADY CAPULET
Juliet!

[She embraces her dead daughter.
Enter LORD MONTAGUE.]

PRINCE
Come, Montague—

MONTAGUE
        --My wife is dead to-night;
Grief of my son's exile hath stopped her breath:
What further woe conspires against mine age?

PRINCE
Look, and thou shalt see.

MONTAGUE
O thou untaught! what manners is in this?
To press before thy father to a grave?

PRINCE
Bring forth the parties of suspicion.
[FRIAR LAWRENCE is brought forward. He is clearly
fearful of the blood and bodies.]
Say at once what thou dost know in this.

FRIAR LAWRENCE
I will be brief...
Romeo, there dead, was husband to that Juliet;
And she, there dead, that Romeo's faithful wife:
I married them; and their stol'n marriage-day
Was Tybalt's dooms-day, whose untimely death
Banished the new-made bridegroom from the city.
To rid her from a second marriage *[indicating PARIS]*
I gave to her a sleeping potion;

26

That wrought on her the form of death: meantime
I writ to Romeo, that he should hither come
To help to take her from her borrowed grave.
But he which bore my letter, Friar John,
Was stayed by Searchers, and so yesternight
Returned my letter back.

PRINCE
Where's Romeo's man? what can he say in this?

BALTHASAR
I brought my master news of Juliet's death;
And then in post he came from Mantua.
This letter he early bid me give his father.

PRINCE *[Taking the letter]*
This letter doth make good the friar's words,
Their course of love, the tidings of her death:
That he did buy a poison, and therewithal
Came to this vault to die, and lie with Juliet.
Where be these enemies? Capulet! Montague!
See, what a scourge is laid upon your hate!

CAPULET
O brother Montague, give me thy hand…

*[CAPULET and MONTAGUE take hands. All are
weeping, embracing. Dawn begins to break.]*

PRINCE ESCALUS
A glooming peace this morning with it brings;
The sun, for sorrow, will not show his head:

Go hence, to have more talk of these sad things;
Some shall be pardoned, and some punished:
For never was a story of more woe
Than this of Juliet and—

*[PRINCE ESCALUS is cut off as a re-animated JULIET
attacks him, biting out his vocal chords. He doesn't finish
his speech. The assembled group is paralyzed with shock,
watching as JULIET savages ESCALUS. He gasps and
gurgles. JULIET spins around to face the others.]*

JULIET
Mother?

*[LADY CAPULET shrieks and chaos erupts. JULIET
stumbles towards her mother, who staggers backwards,
tripping on her skirts.]*

JULIET
Mother? Mother?

*[LORD CAPULET tries to pull his wife out of danger.
FRIAR LAWRENCE is on high alert, in a defensive pose.
BALTHASAR stays with him, as does Paris's PAGE. With
a nod to each other, the SEARCHERS melt into the
background.]*

LADY CAPULET
            Juliet, what hast thou done?

FRIAR LAWRENCE
Touch her not, Lady! A curse is in her blood—

CAPULET
How dare you say that of a Capulet?

MONTAGUE
Was this the family with whom I thought
To make a peace? What worm is in the trunk
If thus the branches be so bitten?
[He snatches up Escalus' fallen crown.]
I'll save the Prince's crown, if not the Prince…

CAPULET
What, Montague, think you to make a claim
Now that the Prince and Paris are no more?
Give me that crown—

[CAPULET and MONTAGUE struggle, fighting over the crown.]

FRIAR LAWRENCE
                              My Lady—Lady! No!

*[JULIET has caught up to her mother and bites her.
LADY CAPULET screams bloody murder. ROMEO sits
up.]*

ROMEO
Juliet?

*[Panic. ROMEO looks around, puzzled. He shakes his
head as though trying to get water out of his ear. He sees
BALTHASAR.]*

ROMEO
Balthasar. I'm hungry.

CAPULET
You see, old hypocrite! T'was your own son
That spread infection to my darling daughter—

MONTAGUE
Your darling daughter has just bitten off
Your wife's left little finger. It was she
Who bit my son!

CAPULET
                        You liar! Reprobate!

FRIAR LAWRENCE
You fools! Have you no eyes? Look to the tomb!

*[ROMEO, still groggy, hasn't gotten up yet. But PARIS
and TYBALT are rising. A fierce light glows in PARIS'
eyes.]*

PARIS
I'll eat you all, you bastards. No one asked
If Paris had his own plans for his life!

*[MONTAGUE and CAPULET flee offstage, still fighting
over the crown as PARIS moves to pursue them.]*

FIRST SEARCHER and SECOND SEARCHER
Halt!

*[The SEARCHERS leap out of hiding, throwing off their
Watch cloaks to reveal themselves: Two women, each
carrying a white wand. They are dressed for fighting the
undead: leather, buckles, high boots, bristling with
weaponry. A comic book nerd's dream.]*

30

FIRST SEARCHER
You! Revenant! Eat this!

*[She takes a running attack at PARIS, and stabs him
through the head. He falls down dead.]*

FRIAR LAWRENCE
The Searchers of the Town! The Lord be praised!

*[He huddles BALTHASAR and the PAGE back out of the
way of the Searchers. The FIRST SEARCHER
approaches PARIS and gives him a kick.]*

SECOND SEARCHER
Dead?

FIRST SEARCHER
        Of course.

SECOND SEARCHER
                    For certain?

FIRST SEARCHER
                                And for sure.

SECOND SEARCHER
What next?

FIRST SEARCHER
        The Prince is stirring.

SECOND SEARCHER
                        Sounds like fun.

[ESCALUS, his throat mauled by JULIET, is rising. The SECOND SEARCHER pivots lightly towards him and salutes, mockingly.]

SECOND SEARCHER
Prince Escalus! Your throat is hanging out.

[She stabs him through the head with her white wand. Meanwhile, the FIRST SEARCHER is taking stock of TYBALT and ROMEO. TYBALT is less befuddled than ROMEO, but where ROMEO seems to have something wrong with his balance, TYBALT is more distracted by things around him. He's admiring the flowers on his tomb, the velvet of his doublet, the way the gloomy morning light moves along the wall of the crypt, the feel of the cold stone. Reawakened, his artistic, beauty-loving soul, repressed in life, is waking up too. The FIRST SEARCHER is not impressed. The SECOND SEARCHER comes to her side.]

FIRST SEARCHER
Finished?

SECOND SEARCHER
                Easy. I never liked him much.

FIRST SEARCHER
Bit of a ponce, I always thought. What's here?

SECOND SEARCHER
Slow wakers. *[a laugh]* We should call the trainees in. You want the Prince of Cats?

FIRST SEARCHER

Why not? And you?

SECOND SEARCHER
I'll do for Romeo.

*[At the sound of his name, JULIET's head wrenches up
from where she's been nibbling at LADY CAPULET. She
wheels around and sees the SEARCHERS advancing on
TYBALT and ROMEO. She launches herself towards
them, throwing the SECOND SEARCHER across the
crypt, knocking her unconscious, and ferociously shoving
the FIRST SEARCHER aside. ROMEO and TYBALT
seem to understand that they should do something, but
they're not sure what. JULIET crouches over ROMEO.]*

JULIET
You'll not touch him! I'll tear you joint by joint!

FIRST SEARCHER
You'll try.

ROMEO [musing]
        "I'll tear you joint by joint"…why should
Those words ring so familiar in mine ears?

*[BALTHASAR startles. FRIAR LAWRENCE pulls at him
urgently, whispering:]*

FRIAR LAWRENCE
Balthasar—come quick. We must leave now.

BALTHASAR
But Friar—he said those very words to me.
Can he remember? Is he still Romeo?

FRIAR LAWRENCE
He's dead and so are we if we remain.
Come! Come! We'll parse this later, Balthasar.

*[FRIAR LAWRENCE, BALTHASAR, and PAGE run off,
leaving the FIRST SEARCHER alone with the risen dead
and her unconscious partner.]*

JULIET
Romeo! Tybalt! Wake and save yourselves!
Or help me bite a way out of the tomb!

ROMEO *[rising, breaking through the fog]*
Breakfast?

TYBALT
                    Breakfast?

LADY CAPULET *[sitting up]*
                              Breakfast?

FIRST SEARCHER
                                        Puttana madre.

*[All four revenants move to attack. The FIRST
SEARCHER grabs the SECOND SEARCHER—slinging
her over a shoulder, if possible, and escapes.
BLACKOUT.]*

ACT II, SCENE 1
Friar Lawrence's cell

[Enter FRIAR LAWRENCE, BALTHASAR, and the PAGE, out of breath and terrified. The FRIAR finds a lamp and lights it.]

BALTHASAR
What happened? Friar, what happened at the tomb?

PAGE
The dead came back to life, Sir Balthasar!
My lord was dead, but then he rose, and walked,
And gaped his jaws wide like a ravening dog
And said that he would eat us! Eat our flesh!

BALTHASAR
Calm thyself, boy. The Friar will make all clear.

PAGE
And Juliet that Paris was to wed
Bit out the life of Escalus the Prince,
And ate her mother after! Romeo
And Tybalt fiended up from certain death
Where they lay patiently upon their tombs
As if they had but slept a good night's sleep—
If corpses rise and walk, and eat us too,
All hope is lost! There's nothing we can do!

FRIAR LAWRENCE
Boy. Be still. Hysteria is your foe—
Not corpses, though they rise, and walk, and eat.

PAGE
But 'tis the plague! 'Tis come from Mantua
Where sorcerers that scorn the laws of heaven
Work fiendish evil on the people there.
They breed diseases—

[FRIAR LAWRENCE slaps the PAGE, who goes quiet.]

FRIAR LAWRENCE
          Silence! I must think.

[He searches through piles of books and papers.]

FRIAR LAWRENCE
Balthasar, you said that Romeo
Spoke certain words to you before
He died and then returned again therefrom.

BALTHASAR
He said he'd tear me limb from limb if I
Should pry into his secret business further.

FRIAR LAWRENCE
A less than friendly saying. Said he this
With any tremors in the voice or body?

BALTHASAR
No Father, but his whole corporal self
Bespoke a fierce determination—
Like one who goes to battle, or to death.

FRIAR LAWRENCE
No trembling. Hmmm. Well did he then complain
Of headache, fever, chills or other such?

BALTHASAR
No Friar.

FRIAR LAWRENCE
                Did he perspire overmuch?
Did his whole forehead bead with sweating drops?

BALTHASAR
We rode hard through the night, from Mantua;
I fear we both had sweated through our shirts.

FRIAR LAWRENCE
And his complexion, was it pale, or greenish?

BALTHASAR
Pale, yes, he was—but then the light was dim—
I think not green, though, father friar.

FRIAR LAWRENCE
                                    Not green,
Fine, not green. Was his breathing shallow then?
His heartbeat, fast?

BALTHASAR
                        Why no. Why ask you this?

FRIAR LAWRENCE
Was there a bite or mark you could discern
Upon his person, anywhere at all?

BALTHASAR
There were no bites, good sir, that I could see.
We came in haste from Mantua, only stopping

37

To write that hasty letter to his father
And snatch up a small vial that he'd purchased
From an apothecary thereabouts—

FRIAR LAWRENCE
Oh Gods.
An apothecary, say you?

BALTHASAR
                    Yes, sir,
A wizened, mean old man, a beggar, sir,
That scarce could walk, and whistled when he laughed
Like kettles on the flame.

FRIAR LAWRENCE
                    Apothecary.
My old apprentice, now I see your hand
And in its work the evil that you've done.
My boys, this is no mild and passing plague
That threatens our sweet town, and sweeter souls:
I should have known the agent, and the cause
When Juliet first sat up in the tomb.
[To the PAGE] Your fear is well-placed, son. Now
quickly, come!
Take you these books, and Balthasar, that lamp.

PAGE
Why should I carry books? What's going on?

FRIAR LAWRENCE
Boy! We have no time for chit-chat! Pick them up!

BALTHASAR
Friar, please, you must not hide from us
The secrets that you seem to know! Tell us
What happened to my friend and to his love?
And to her mother and the Prince and Count!

FRIAR LAWRENCE
There is no time, the pestilence will spread
Unless we nip it in the bud, and cut it off.
It may already be too late to stop it—
[They look at him, insistent.]
I'll sum it up, in brief: this is a scourge,
Created by a man that I once taught
He studied drugs I would not teach him of;
The last I knew he sailed into the West,
In search of evil plants and deadly spells,
But now I fear that he has come back home,
And Romeo fall'n victim to his wares.
Th'infection spreads through bites and through the blood
I think—though this is speculation—
[The glass of a windowpane shatters at the side wall.
Moaning is heard and filthy hands push through the frame.]

FRIAR LAWRENCE
Oh god, 'tis starting. Quick! Stand back, you fool!

[BALTHASAR pulls out a short sword and slices off one of
the hands. We hear a blood-curdling scream and the other
hand retreats. BALTHASAR thinks for a split second, then
stabs out the window in the direction of the unseen
creature's head. He stabs hard. The noise stops. With a
rough yank, BALTHASAR pulls his sword back into the
room. There is a dripping piece of brain stuck on it.]

39

BALTHASAR
…Good my lords. I've brained him.

FRIAR LAWRENCE
So it would seem you have. Now touch it not!
[He puts the brain sample into a small container.]
A quick sword is a fine weapon, sir, when
Wall and windowframe assist the bearer.
Do not now fool yourself, to think these wights
Will always be so easy to destroy.
[Looking out the window.]
It was a good stab, howsoe'er. Well…placed.

BALTHASAR
Thanks, Friar. You think the Apothecary
Of Mantua is the maker of this terror?

FRIAR LAWRENCE
I fear he is.

BALTHASAR
                    It spreads by bites, you think?

FRIAR LAWRENCE
I fear it does. But it begins with drugs
Poisons foully mixed, that kill the brain—
Administered with terrible intent.
Shhh!

*[A guttural moaning is heard outside. The FRIAR blows
out the lamp and the three crouch in tense silence as more
shambling figures move slowly past the window. After
they have passed, BALTHASAR looks out cautiously.]*

BALTHASAR
…I don't see any more, for now.

FRIAR LAWRENCE
I thought him gone forever, when he left:
But now I see the evil in his nature
Has triumphed o'er the good. I'll study this:
It will take precious time, but if I can
Detect in it a poisonous residue,
I can find out a way to fight this plague.

BALTHASAR
I've seen his shop in Mantua. Would he not
Have kept a book, or records of his potions,
Some clue to speed us? In two hours I can
Be there and back again. I'll search his papers,
Steal what evidence I can—

FRIAR LAWRENCE
                                        Balthasar:
Do it. You'll find us in my laboratory.
Ride swift, and may god bless and ride with thee.
[To the Page] Now quickly, gather up these necessaries
And haste we in our several directions.
If you see more of these creatures, stab quick:
Through the brainpan seems the surest way.
And Balthasar—

BALTHASAR
                        My lord?

FRIAR LAWRENCE
                                        Don't let them bite you.
[They exit.]

41

ACT II, SCENE 2
The Capulet tomb in the graveyard

ROMEO
Juliet?

JULIET
    Romeo?

BOTH
                I had thought thee dead.

JULIET
Thou wert dead, good my lord, I saw thy corpse:
Thou drankest deadly poison and dropped down
Upon my tomb.

ROMEO
             Thy tomb where thou laidst dead!
I saw thee, Juliet—thou wast dead first.
I drank the poison that I might join thee.

JULIET
I was not dead, but only sleeping dead.

ROMEO
Well sleeping dead looked dead enough to me.
I would you'd told me of your plan to play
This ghostly farce before I killed myself,
My love, for grief at your dear loss.

JULIET
You might have had a bit more patience, love,
Before you oh-so-swiftly offed yourself.

42

But five more minutes, I had been alive,
With you, and not at all stabbed through the heart.

ROMEO
Who stabbed you? Was it I? I don't think so.
I rather think your own hand struck that blow.

JULIET
Because I saw you dead!

ROMEO
                              Well you died first!

[They exclaim in frustration. A pause.]

ROMEO
I'm sorry that I killed myself so soon.

JULIET
I'm sorry that I was not truly dead.
They wanted me to marry Paris, though;
And Friar said he'd tell you and the drug
He gave me would wear off in time
For you to take me off to Mantua.

ROMEO
I heard from Balthasar that you were dead
And all I wanted was to be with you.

[TYBALT is moved.]

TYBALT
O! It is so beautiful!

[ROMEO and JULIET look at each other. This is not the TYBALT they are used to.]

JULIET
Tybalt? Cousin? Are you well?

TYBALT
Well I am dead, but that's not why I weep—
O heavens, O you two! 'Tis all too much!
I never knew you loved each other, truly,
I am a trifle overwhelmed. Forgive me.
[he sobs, overcome. Romeo approaches him awkwardly]

ROMEO
Ah, Tybalt, dear Tybalt, my cousin, now…
[He looks to JULIET for reassurance; she nods encouragingly.]
This is perhaps not the best time to say it,
But I am very sorry that I killed you.
I was upset about Mercutio—
That's no excuse for murder; I know that—
But since we're family now, and, well, un-dead,
Can you forgive me, and a peace be made?

TYBALT
O, Romeo. In life
I was a killer, indiscriminate;
Quick to umbrage, quick to anger, so swift
To pour my rage in to the silver point
Of my quick-cutting sword. I hope,
Since in the book of Tybalt I am given
To turn another leaf, I shall not be
So swift to act in anger. Nor shall I

Stint forgiveness. Within my breast and in
The world around me, I crave peace
As does a newborn babe desire to breathe.
I forgive you, Romeo, 'tis all bygones.
I am the one who's sorry, to you both.
In truth it was not me. Let us start fresh.
[he takes a deep cleansing breath]
Juliet, I must say, death becomes you!

JULIET *[flattered, a bit shy]*
O, thank you Tybalt. You look...quite nice too.

[TYBALT, having been dead a few days and then splattered with Juliet's blood, does not look exactly "quite nice," but let it go, let it go, he's turning over a new leaf.]

TYBALT
So! What are we to do, now that we're dead!
Or is that what we are? I am not sure.

ROMEO
I'm pretty sure I died. I drank the drug
That old apothecary gave to me.

JULIET
I know I died. *[She indicates the dagger in her heart.]*
                         This sort of thing
Is usually rather permanent.

TYBALT
Well kittens, what's to do? *[He gets a sudden thought.]*
                         Are we in heaven?

JULIET
No. We can't be. Where are all the angels?

ROMEO
I see an angel, here.

JULIET
                        O, Romeo. *[She blushes, as*
far as that's possible.]

TYBALT
Stop it, you two, you'll make me cry again.
[He gets another sudden idea.]
What if we're in...the other place?
[They all look around, this time a bit frightened.]

JULIET
How would we know?

TYBALT
                        How could we know? *[gasping:]*
Oh go-o-od!

[He has seen LADY CAPULET, who enters, gnawing on a
dismembered body part. Something unexpected and
gruesome...perhaps a knee. She has been doing some
serious flesh eating since the morning's bloodbath.
TYBALT's gasp breaks her concentration and she looks
up at him.]

LADY CAPULET
Oh, Tybalt! Are you hungry, darling boy?
[She holds the joint out to him. He demurs.]
Not hungry? Well, that's all the more for me!

I cannot tell you what a lovely thing
It is to feast without restraint! I never
was a glutton—Far from it!
In fact, I'd sooner fast, and know for sure
My girlish gowns would still fit as they did
When I was married. Now I find, however,
That vanity is boring. Better, far,
To do the things that I would like to do.
[She takes a great big bite.]
Oh, rapture. *[A steely, foxy light comes into her eyes.]*
Have you seen your father, Juliet?

JULIET
No, Mother...

LADY CAPULET
          Well, I'll find him soon enough.
Tybalt, eat! You need your nourishment.

*[She throws the joint to TYBALT, who shrieks and fumbles
the bloody thing as LADY CAPULET heads off, licking
her chops, smoothing her hair and straightening her
bloody gown. TYBALT hurls the joint towards one of the
other two, and a brief tossing game of *I don't want it—
you take it!* erupts. This ends when JULIET, about to
pass it on, hesitates, her appetite whetted. Tentatively,
she sniffs it. She sniffs a second time.]*

JULIET
Would you now think me rude, if I should have
The tiniest little bite? I find I'm not
So disinclined as one might think I ought
To be, to taste this juicy, bloody...knee?

47

ROMEO *[equally intrigued]*
Is it a knee? I've never had a knee!
Is that a tendon? I wonder how that tastes…

TYBALT *[queasy]*
Dear cousin, and dear…cousin, I'll…away.
I fear my stomach is not quite at ease
With your repast. Forgive me—I'll go walk.
The grounds are lovely, hereabouts. Enjoy…
[They make one last offer of the joint, which he waves off.]
No. As my Lady Aunt says, more for you!

*[TYBALT heads off quickly among the tombs. ROMEO
and JULIET begin feeding each other, in the most courtly,
sweet, puppy-love style, pieces of the bloody leg in their
hands.]*

ROMEO
My sweetling, would you like a little nibble?

JULIET
Why yes, my lord, a nibble would please me well.

ROMEO
Then you shall have one! Woe betide the man
Who dares deny my love her nibble!

JULIET
                                                            O!

'Tis ever so delicious. Love, would you
Enjoy a chewy little bite? From me,
To you?

ROMEO
                O yes! But feed me little bites,
And I am yours, and paradise is ours!

*[JULIET lovingly pulls a strip of flesh off the bone and
sweetly feeds one end of it to ROMEO so that they have
one end of it in each of their mouths, a la Lady and the
Tramp. There they are, on either end of a meat strand,
chewing their way towards each other, still holding the
leg between them. They are close to kissing. TYBALT calls
to them, entering.]*

TYBALT
Cousins, Mercutio's tomb is empty! Oh.
Ahem, excuse me! There's an empty tomb
That housed Mercutio's corpse, but now
He's gone.

[The SEARCHERS re-appear.]

FIRST SEARCHER
                You'll be gone soon enough, dead man.

SECOND SEARCHER *[Pointing at TYBALT, ROMEO,
and JULIET in order.]*
Gone, goner, gonest. Quite a trio, sister.

TYBALT
You need not draw your weapons on us, ladies,
We mean no harm—

FIRST SEARCHER
                Can't say the same of us.

[She attacks. TYBALT, still the King of Cats, evades her, but takes a blow on the arm.]

TYBALT
Ah! ...You. Tore. My. Sleeve.

[TYBALT is not pleased. They fight. The SECOND SEARCHER squares off with ROMEO, who places JULIET behind him. They fight.]

ROMEO
Why wave your weapon at me? I am not
Your enemy.

SECOND SEARCHER
　　　　　Sister, why are they talking?

FIRST SEARCHER
I know not—Ah!

[TYBALT has disarmed her and presses his advantage. The SECOND SEARCHER runs to deflect a deadly blow. ROMEO turns quickly to JULIET.]

ROMEO
I'll draw them off.
Get thee to safety while I rescue Tybalt.

JULIET
I will not leave thee. I can help. I'll fight.

ROMEO
My love I cannot watch you risk your life.

[TYBALT's luck has turned and the two SEARCHERS are getting the better of him. He cries out.]

ROMEO
Nor can I watch as he is killed again--
To safety, go! Where you asked what's in a name—
I'll find you there!

JULIET
                    My love—

ROMEO
                              I'll find you. Run!

[JULIET turns and runs. ROMEO joins the fight, and he and TYBALT overpower the SEARCHERS long enough to make their escape and exit.]

SECOND SEARCHER
Jesu Christe!

FIRST SEARCHER
        I do not like it that they talked.
Let's go. You follow them. I'll track the girl.
[She prepares to pursue JULIET.]

SECOND SEARCHER
Wait, sister—I don't know if we should fight them.
These three are not at all the same as those
We're sworn to kill.

FIRST SEARCHER
                    They're dead and risen, aren't they?

SECOND SEARCHER
Yes, but—

FIRST SEARCHER
          Come on. They're getting away.

*[The SECOND SEARCHER exits. The FIRST
SEARCHER watches her leave, then, instead of following
JULIET, melts into the background.]*

ACT II, SCENE 3
Verona: The graveyard

[Later that day. The skies are dark and gloomy. Enter the
APOTHECARY with a young BOY. As he speaks, he casts
a ritual circle on the ground.]

APOTHECARY
There are some things a man may know. And some
A man can know. And things there are that can
Be learned, or taught, or made, but should not be,
Or so men say. Should not. Ought not. May not.
What comfortable lies they tell, these men
Who think it is their job to guide us all
And keep us safe from harm. What childish lies.
There is no should!
There is what can be done and what is done.
Why should we fear to do the things we can?
Nature brews us poisons—why? To test us?
No. No! There is no "Nature!" No goddess,
No god, no truth, no law, no public good;
No benevolent master, guiding us
So that we never slip, nor fall, nor fail.
But look around, and see: if we are guided,
Our guide is not the best. Our kings and princes
Fail us, every day. The people die
The good man suffers, the kind are trod upon,
The rich buy up the powerful in secret
And wield their puppets with impunity;
Diseases and the gallows both devour
The innocent without a second thought—
Not even a first. Why play this game wherein
Belief ascribes a motive to the world,

When every scrap of evidence we see
Proclaims the truth aloud: There is no plan!
There is no order! No one is in charge!
Do what you will, we swim in chaos, child.
Throw off the yoke and tyranny of belief!
Suffer no more the angst and the betrayal:
But understand that life is as we make it,
And all resentment slides away like ice.
Bring out the creature.
[The BOY goes into one of the tombs. A heavy chain is
heard, dragging.]
Slave! Come forth!
[A large figure drags in heavily from the back, the BOY
leading him. This creature is in the traditional vein:
unable to speak, less in control of his movement,
completely in thrall to his maker, the APOTHECARY.
The BOY leads the creature into the circle, which the
APOTHECARY closes.]
Ah, good. Now stay there, slave!
[The APOTHECARY gingerly examines the creature, who
is slumped over and very still.]
I once believed in justice, and in gods,
And that good men could teach me right from wrong:
How wrong was I, to trust them with my youth!
I wrenched it back though, ere they ate it all;
Not like you: your friends ate you, life and all.
I took the strength I had and boarded ship:
For months I sailed after the setting sun,
I swabbed hard decks and shriveled in my skin,
I huddled down below while tempests raged
And great waves rocked our ship, and fearsome beasts
Swam up from down below to glare at us
And munch the bones of those unlucky few

Who fell. I endured all, and when we landed
I found in that new land far meeter subjects
For my appetites. I sought the lairs
Of jungle sorcerers, and conned their secrets.
I'll tell you plain—since you will never speak
To others of it—I stole their knowledge.
Even they had rules they bid me follow,
But I am not a follower of rules.
What they would not give willingly, I took.
Of potions and of simples and of powders
Their mastery has no equal in this land.
I learned the devil's trumpet, and the weeds
That stop the tongue and paralyze the limbs;
I sought the deadly moonflower, and found
The desert thorn-apple that blooms by night;
I snared the sugartoad, and tasted death
In its fishy spines: the cook must taste the soup.
I am not quite as pretty as I was,
But learning has its price, and I learned much.
Come hither, boy. There is a thing that I
Must test. Dost fear to die?

BOY
                              Aye, my lord.

APOTHECARY
                                        Why?

BOY
                              I know not, my lord.
Everyone fears death.

55

APOTHECARY

                           That creature whose chain
You hold, he's dead—ah, drop it not, my boy.
Didst enjoy thy dinner? Thou atest mightily.

BOY
I did, sir. I was very hungry.

APOTHECARY
No doubt you had not eaten for some time.
Poverty, famine, desperation...
I mean to feed you to this dead man here.

BOY
Oh, no, my lord, please, I would rather not.

APOTHECARY
Hush. Either he will eat you, and you'll die,
Or you will die and then become like him.
It is a thing that I must try, and you,
My lad, cannot imagine that you'll be
Worse off than starving, orphaned, and alone.
Perhaps death will be nice. Hold out your arm.

*[The BOY does so. The APOTHECARY grasps the arm
and holds it out to the creature.]*

APOTHECARY
Feed.

*[The creature bites. The BOY screams, convulses, and
goes limp. Seconds tick by.]*

56

APOTHECARY
Now we shall see how swift my plague can move—
Will't creep, while corpse by corpse I make them mine,
Or exponentially o'ertake the land?

*[The BOY re-animates. He snaps upright and lets out a
thin, high-pitched wail. The APOTHECARY is pleased.]*

APOTHECARY
The quick way, then.

*[He throws a heavy sack over the BOY, who falls,
twitching. With a terrifying sound, the larger creature
lashes out, sudden and savage. The APOTHECARY leaps
out of range, just barely. He yanks the chain around the
creature's neck, pulling him back and down. The creature
pants and glares.]*

APOTHECARY
No, no, no, no, my lad, we'll none of that.
You mind your manners or I'll break your leg
Off at the knee. Hobbled Mercutio,
The sad, dead slave.
[A noise]
                                                Who's there?
*[A shadowy figure appears near the crypts. It is the FIRST
SEARCHER, though this is not evident at first.]*

FIRST SEARCHER
You sent a messenger from Mantua.

APOTHECARY *[extremely cautious]*
I…did.

FIRST SEARCHER
    Your message carried a request.

APOTHECARY
It did.

FIRST SEARCHER
    You asked that certain special tools
Be brought to you, in Verona, today.

APOTHECARY
You try my patience. What is the reply?

*[A threatening sound—perhaps a crossbow being set or a
sword drawn. MERCUTIO stirs. The Apothecary flinches
instinctively. Low laughter filters coldly from the gloom.
A wrapped parcel lands at the APOTHECARY'S feet.]*

FIRST SEARCHER
A gift. Call it that.

[The SEARCHER steps into the light, revealing herself.]

APOTHECARY
                        Ah, my searcher friend!
I hoped it would be you.

*[The APOTHECARY snatches up the parcel and opens it.
He brings out a thimbleful of powder and blows it in
MERCUTIO'S face. MERCUTIO roars, flails as if
against flying enemies, gags, chokes, and finally subsides
into catatonic dullness. The APOTHECARY pets him
sadistically.]*

APOTHECARY
There, that is better now.

FIRST SEARCHER
Such a creature should not walk on the earth.
Shall I kill it for you?

APOTHECARY *[friendly]*
                                        Should you do that,
I'll rip your heart out and feed you your own blood.

[A silence.]

FIRST SEARCHER
It cannot speak, your creature?

APOTHECARY
                                        No, the drug
Thickens the tongue, and eats away the brains.
Is it not so, my pretty sword-pricked lad?

FIRST SEARCHER
I've seen those as speak.

APOTHECARY
                        What?

FIRST SEARCHER
                                        The risen dead.
I've seen some that can speak.

APOTHECARY

A fantasy.

You've spent too long in darkness. Or perhaps
You sampled some of my forbidden wares?

FIRST SEARCHER
I eat no pills nor suck no potions, friend.
I heard the dead talk princely as you please,
And killed a few for lacking due respect.
But speak they did. Be warned, Apothecary,
There's evil work afoot, and not your own.

[A pause.]

APOTHECARY
Who? What dead spoke to you?

FIRST SEARCHER

Have you my payment?

APOTHECARY
I thought this was a gift?
[The FIRST SEARCHER shrugs and turns to go.]

No wait—your fee.

[He tosses a small pouch of coins, which the FIRST
SEARCHER pockets.]

FIRST SEARCHER
The Capulet girl. And her cousin Tybalt.
And Romeo, the Montague, who died
This morning in the graveyard.

APOTHECARY

                                        Say you so?

If that be true it is unlooked for news.
I would I could count you secure in my
Employ. Have you thought further on my offer?

FIRST SEARCHER
Have you thought further upon mine to you?
Gold is nice, but power is better far.
Knowledge is better: come what may, one keeps it.
[She indicates the moneypouch.]
My fealty is not so cheaply bought.

APOTHECARY
My mentorship is not so cheaply won.
I know not if this tale you tell be true;
But if you bring these creatures to me, I'll pay
More than that little fee you have in hand.

FIRST SEARCHER
If I snare your rabbits, will you teach me
That which I desire to know?

APOTHECARY

                                        Come tonight,

With speaking corpses for me, and we'll see.
Wait! Have you found it?

FIRST SEARCHER

                                        What?

APOTHECARY

Whatever it is
You're searching for. *[He laughs. She waits.]* I jest.
But what of your companion? Is she still
Asking irksome questions?

FIRST SEARCHER

She knows nothing.

APOTHECARY
She must know something.

FIRST SEARCHER

Nothing about this.

[The BOY stirs, hidden by the bag.]

FIRST SEARCHER
What's that?

APOTHECARY

Not your concern. Come back tonight.

*[The FIRST SEARCHER hesitates, then nods, and
vanishes. The BOY stirs again.]*

APOTHECARY
Pick it up. Come on, slave,
I have a new quarry for you to hunt:
Juliet Capulet…dead or alive.

[The APOTHECARY, MERCUTIO, and BOY exit.]

ACT III, SCENE 1

Verona: the house of the SEARCHERS, Later that afternoon.

[The SECOND SEARCHER enters warily, spattered with blood and gore. Satisfied that the house is empty, she relaxes, testing her body for bruises, injuries. Hearing a noise, she whirls around, wand up. It is the FIRST SEARCHER.]

FIRST SEARCHER
So. Did you kill them?

SECOND SEARCHER
                              No, I lost the trail.
Romeo jumped the wall into the orchard
And Tybalt ducked away and ran for town.
I killed five others though, that came for me.
The kind that do not talk. The kind that bite.
D'you still think the end times are not here?

FIRST SEARCHER
I do not know.

[She goes to a shelf and takes down a musical instrument, which she strums at distractedly.]

SECOND SISTER
                              Play us a song, sister.

FIRST SEARCHER
Why do you always call me sister? We're not
Sisters.

SECOND SEARCHER
           We are. Not of the blood, but of
The heart. Of the quest. Of the journey.

FIRST SEARCHER
                              Ah.

*[A pause. The FIRST SEARCHER continues to pluck
notes out of the strings, without making eye contact with
the SECOND SEARCHER.]*

SECOND SEARCHER
Sing, please.

FIRST SEARCHER
                    Alright. I'll sing.
[SONG — A Lullabye]
Hush, darling, hush dear
Though nighttime be near
You need never fear
For I will be here
And I will not leave you alone

The crows they are calling, the wind it blows fierce
The candles are flickering low
Our lives are a little, a little bright time
And sooner or later, we go

But hush darling, hush dear
Though nighttime be near
You need never fear
For I will be here
And I will not leave you alone

We ride through the hours and over the seasons
The spin and the arc of the world:
Our lives are a little, a little bright time
So hush and be happy, my girl

Hush darling, hush dear
Though nighttime be near
You need never fear
For I am right here
And I will not leave you alone

[Silence.]

FIRST SEARCHER
I don't know why I sang that one.

SECOND SEARCHER
I think the end is coming. It is good.
I do not fear to die in thy company.

FIRST SEARCHER
Who said anything about dying?

SECOND SEARCHER
                                                    Oh, death
Is all around us. I know not, if when
I took the Searcher's path, I thought it would
Be me to fight the battle, me to face
The final, awful scourge. But here I am,
I took my vows. I'll fight against the darkness,
And if I cannot stop it, yet will I
Tax its forces mightily ere I go.

FIRST SEARCHER
You need not die. What if there were a way—
Another way, another path, a sturdier
Allegiance—

*[The SECOND SEARCHER looks at her sharply, beset by
deep suspicion, puzzle pieces sliding into place. They
hold each other's gaze. Finally the FIRST SEARCHER
laughs, too loudly.]*

                              Only testing, Sister.
I'm glad to see the coward's way has no
Allure for you. We'll fight like furies if
This is the end. I think 'tis not, but I'll
Be ready if it is.

SECOND SEARCHER
                    The city's thick
With walking corpses, and 'tis growing thicker.
Perhaps we should seek help from San Martino,
Or Grezzana. We need not fight alone.

FIRST SEARCHER
There is no need for outside help. I'll take
The graveyard on my own tonight, and you
Can manage any trouble in the town.
Unless you think you can't?

SECOND SEARCHER
                              I'll manage it.

FIRST SEARCHER
A storm is rising. We'll have thunder soon.

SECOND SEARCHER
What is Verona in July without
A thunderstorm?

FIRST SEARCHER
                    Those clouds will bring the night
Down sooner, too.

SECOND SEARCHER
                    Our work is done at night.
We'll start the sooner. [*A grinding crack of thunder.*]

FIRST SEARCHER
                              Let's start it now.

[*The FIRST SEARCHER stands to go. About to exit, she
turns back and embraces the SECOND SEARCHER
fiercely.*]

Be safe, sister. Be strong.

[*Just as swiftly, she breaks the embrace and exits without
looking back. The SECOND SEARCHER exits more
slowly, in the opposite direction.*]

ACT III, SCENE 2
Juliet's balcony, now unpeopled

[Night is falling. High winds have begun to blow, the rumbling thunder coming closer. JULIET enters, terrified and trying to stay hidden. She looks up at the balcony.]

JULIET
Romeo?
Art thou there? Hist! Romeo, hist!

[She pulls herself up a bit towards the balcony, craning to see if he is up there. A sudden sound from the orchard snaps her attention around, and she slides down and ventures out into the open space below the balcony. Not able to see well in the dark, she moves forward cautiously.]

JULIET
Hallo? Who's there? Romeo? ...Tybalt?

[A flash of lightning reveals the stage—empty save for JULIET—in stark relief. She startles, then tries to calm herself as a grinding crack of thunder follows.]

JULIET
I am alone. Alone. There's no one here.

[Lightning. In the second flash of light, we see a hulking figure, standing motionless in upstage silhouette. Then everything is dark again. We see JULIET's face glowing in an eerie pinlight, far downstage, peering out into the darkness.]

JULIET
I am the first one here. Or they have come
And gone, while I was hiding from the creatures
In the street. Hush—Romeo will come.

*[Silently, the huge figure begins moving towards
JULIET.]*

JULIET
Romeo come quick. Come quick, my love—

*[Another flash of lightning. JULIET spins around and
sees the figure, almost within arm's reach of her. She
leaps back—then recognizes him. It is MERCUTIO. He
is still for a moment, then begins moving towards JULIET
again, inexorably.]*

JULIET
Mercutio? Mercutio? Is't you?
Are you returned from death?
*[MERCUTIO keeps moving towards her. She backs
away.]*
                              O,
I was so frightened, but you are a friend,
Are you not? Mercutio? Mercutio?

*[JULIET stumbles, tripping over her own feet.
MERCUTIO keeps pursuing her, growing more intent,
more fearsome. JULIET scrambles backwards.
MERCUTIO grabs her and she screams, struggling.]*

JULIET
Help! Romeo!

[Struggling to get away, JULIET claws her way to the balcony, trying to climb out of the MERCUTIO's reach. He pulls her down, screaming and struggling. He bites her.

There is a sudden change in MERCUTIO. He drops the struggling JULIET, who scrambles away from him. He jerks unnaturally. He swallows. He collapses. JULIET approaches the body.]

JULIET
...Mercutio?

[He doesn't move. She strokes his head, and gently turns the body over so it is resting in her lap.]

O, my poor friend.

[MERCUTIO's arm shoots up and grabs her by the neck. She gasps. Then just as suddenly the hand relaxes. Gently, MERCUTIO touches her face. In a ragged voice, he says:]

MERCUTIO
Juliet?

[She nods, still unsure of whether or not he's dangerous. He strokes her cheek, touches a lock of hair, and pulls her into a kiss. Surprised, she pulls away.]

JULIET
Oh you mustn't!
I know you are confused, but you can't kiss me.
It is…improper. I—

[It is not clear if MERCUTIO can understand her or not.
Still foggy, he moves in to kiss her again. She stops him.]

JULIET
No. Mercutio stay. Good boy.

[MERCUTIO puts his hands up like paws and pants.
Then he shakes his head as though beset by a buzzing
sound he can't stop hearing. His eyes clear and he
flinches, reaching for the stab wound in his side.
Alarmed, he examines his torso, arms...]

MERCUTIO
Where am I?

JULIET
                    In Verona.

MERCUTIO
                              Are you sure?
My mind is foggy. I was stabbed...we fought...
Tybalt, and Romeo...and then, the dark.
A fever, and a madness, or a dream...

[He reaches for JULIET, trying to understand what's
happened. He is struck by her body's complete lack of
human warmth.]

You're very cold.

JULIET
                    Well I am dead. We both are.
O sir forgive me; would it were not so,

Or I were defter of my tongue to tell you.
We are dead, yes, but animate—
You died when Tybalt stabbed you, then Romeo
Killed Tybalt, then they banished Romeo,
Then tried to make me marry county Paris,
But I was married first to Romeo,
So Friar Lawrence gave to me a drug
That made me seem dead. Next thing that I knew,
I woke up in my tomb to find my love—
My Romeo—a suicide by poison,
His head a cold weight lying in my lap.
He had not left enough poison for me.
Instead I stabbed myself. I bled a lot,
And then I died.

MERCUTIO
                          But you're not dead.
JULIET
                                            Oh yes,
I'm dead. But now I'm undead. So are you.

MERCUTIO
This is something new.

*[JULIET nods. She winces, and gently feels the back of
her neck where MERCUTIO bit her.]*

MERCUTIO
                                   What happened?

JULIET
Oh—you bit me.

MERCUTIO
                    I bit you?

JULIET
                                        Yes, just now?
You came out of the shadows and attacked?

MERCUTIO
Madness and a dream indeed. Forgive me.

JULIET
Of course! In truth I don't feel any pain
At all. *[She gestures to her neck. An awkward pause.]*

MERCUTIO
                    You married Romeo?

JULIET
Yes. I love him.

MERCUTIO
                    You just met him.

JULIET
                                        I know!
And yet he is my heart's own heart, my love
So true that even death fell down before it.

MERCUTIO
Are you sure? Did you consider your options?
Do you consider them now? Juliet,
Consider me.

JULIET
                    What?

MERCUTIO
Think on me, sweet jewel; if you're giving favors
Why not some for me? I'm so very good
At being grateful. And you know me well.
I've been your family's guest so many times,
You think I never caught your sidelong looks?
I often thought, were I to choose a girl,
A certain Capulet would be the one.

JULIET
I'm married to a Montague.

MERCUTIO
                                          So what?
He's dead. You get a second chance. With me.

JULIET
But I don't love you. I love Romeo.

MERCUTIO
Not Romeo. Not he. You never loved that boy,
That velvet lad, that Montague in lace.
'Tis me you want, sweet Juliet, not him.
You're drawn to me, you crave me, even now—
For I am all the bad boys of your dreams;
The man who'll take your hand and teach you things
Your nurse would never tell you, all those things
You dreamed about, the secrets of your heart
And other places;
What a pale man is Romeo, when you
Compare him to the scarlet of my soul.
And now that everything is changed, why should
You not be free to change your choice as well?
I'm better than your Romeo, you'll see:
Forget his candle—burn the torch of me.

74

JULIET
Mercutio, I wish I had the words
To quell your fervor, though to speak the truth
The words you've spoke are not without effect:
But I love Romeo! I love him!
I killed myself for him, and he for me--
Double-suicide and re-animation
Creates a bond that is too hard to break.

MERCUTIO
I'll find a way.

JULIET
                    Mercutio, enough.

*[ROMEO enters in such a way that MERCUTIO sees him,
but JULIET does not. MERCUTIO locks eyes with him.]*

MERCUTIO
Perhaps your Romeo would like to share.
He got me killed; and we were bosom friends.
I think 'tis not too much to say he owes me.
If pretty Juliet would like to play,
Why should we three not have a little sport?

JULIET
I do not understand just what you mean
But what I comprehend is scandalous—
There are laws, and rules, and…guidelines, all
Instructing us that such things are not right—

MERCUTIO
What's right? We're dead! Let's have a little fun!
My good friend Romeo, when still alive
Ne'er shied away from revelry at hand.

ROMEO
Romeo never had his true love pawed
By friends of doubtful motive.

JULIET
                                        Romeo!
Your friend has said the strangest things to me.

ROMEO
I see he has. And here my other friend
Has listened to them all.

JULIET
                                        Oh, you mistake.
I heard but little, and that little was enough.

ROMEO
To make you blush? To turn your dead cheek scarlet?
I thought you loved me, sweet, but was I wrong?
Do you prefer Mercutio's advances
To my all honest love?

JULIET
                                    O no, my love:
I could not meet you sooner: to escape
The hungry fiends that walk now in the streets,
I hid— t'was nearly night, and storming 'fore
I could with safety travel, but I came
Here to find you, and then I was attacked—
Mercutio attacked me—

ROMEO
                            What?!

JULIET
                              I'm fine!
He was not yet himself. He's changed; he's now
Like us. But when he bit me—

ROMEO
                              Bit you?!

JULIET
                              Yes—

MERCUTIO
I don't remember biting her, I don't.

JULIET
Once he had bitten me, he let me go
And shook, and changed back to himself.

ROMEO
And then assailed you in another way.

MERCUTIO
All that I really did was kiss her once.

ROMEO
You kissed her? You kissed him? And did you like it?

JULIET
I don't know! O Romeo, I love thee!
Believe me, my sweet tassel-gentle,
I am all yours.

ROMEO

                    And I, a peregrine
Too fierce on seeing his mistress feed
Another bird. Lady, I seek only
To give you happiness. Do you prefer
My friend to me?

JULIET

                    No, beloved. Never.
[Indicating her heart, then his:]
Your home is here, mine here.
A visitor is not a resident.

ROMEO
But if you want some other thing--

MERCUTIO

                    Oh peace, oh peace.
Yes, she loves you, she rebuffed me, you win—
You're truly matched, and I will no more meddle.
Your earnestness is safe from me, my loves.

ROMEO
Do you roll your eyes at me, Mercutio?

MERCUTIO
I do, sir, I do roll my eyes at you!
What of it? You love each other: Bravo!
Now please, settle down, settle down, and read
Books to each other of an evening—
There'll be no children of the body, true,
But perhaps you'll have a child of the tooth!
A well-placed bite could make your dreams come true!
But settle down. Heavens forefend you should

78

Escape the cage that held you all your life,
And ask, what are the rules? Are they the same
As they were when I was not dead, and free?
So settle, please. I'll take myself away
To fairer, freer pastures, there to play.

ROMEO
Mercutio, wait.

JULIET
                        Yes please don't leave us now.

ROMEO
I wish you'd stay, and not take such offense
That I prefer to keep my Juliet
Unshared. For now at least! 'Tis only been
A week since we were married, and we've only
Spent one night together. One perfect night...

JULIET
'Tis still our honeymoon! But I don't want
To be old-fashioned all the time... Perhaps
Once Romeo and I have had more time
To share each other with each other, we
Will want to share with someone else as well.
And then who better than my true love's truest
Friend?

ROMEO
        Generous Juliet, but hold my hand
And I'll try anything.

JULIET
                        O Romeo,
If you love me, I'll try anything too.

MERCUTIO
You two are ridiculous.
And yet I love you both. Dear friends, forgive
My mockery. I only wish I had
A friend to pair me as you pair each other.

ROMEO
We'll find you one, my brother. It is good
To see your strong-garrisoned heart open
Its gates, and hear you say that love is not
A thing to be derided only.

MERCUTIO
                                        It is not.
But I have always guarded hard against it.
I've come a long, rough journey since we last
Jested at love's expense.

JULIET
                                        So have we all.
[A beat.]

ROMEO
What happened to you? You were in your grave.

MERCUTIO
I have no memory. Just flashes of
A nightmare. Choking, a chain, a dark cloud
Flooding my mind, my sight, my spirit.
A man—there was a man who poisoned me—
A wheezing, evil man— *[He makes the distinctive sound
of the APOTHECARY breathing/ laughing.]*

ROMEO
I've heard that sound. An apothecary—
I bought a poison from him in Mantua.

MERCUTIO
Now I do bethink me, the surgeon who
Was summoned to my side when I was stabbed—
[He repeats the sound.]
The very same! He was there when I died.

JULIET
                                        And there when you
Came back again from death.

[They look at each other, frightened.]

The Friar. He can tell us what to do.
Where's Tybalt?

MERCUTIO
                    Tybalt?

JULIET
                    [explaining] He is undead too.

ROMEO
We split up to foil the Searchers.

JULIET
But he is very different than he was.

*[A sound. They press themselves into the background,
both ROMEO and MERCUTIO careful to protect JULIET.*

Juliet's NURSE shambles on, undead: slow, ravenous, terrifying. JULIET tenses, and starts towards her. ROMEO stays her, shaking his head no. Swiftly, silently, ROMEO, JULIET, and MERCUTIO move to exit. Just before they make it offstage, JULIET breaks away, calling softly, "Nurse?" The creature stops abruptly. ROMEO pulls Juliet away and the three sprint offstage. The NURSE turns sharply and shambles after them with hungry purpose.]

ACT III, SCENE 3
Verona: a street (continuous)

[Night has settled inexorably over Verona. The city glitters darkly in the wake of the summer thunderstorm. BALTHASAR enters, breathing rapidly after his hard ride to Mantua and back. He carries an evil-looking book. He moves with utmost caution.]

BALTHASAR
The road twixt Mantua and here is crawling.
They took my horse a mile without the town;
I had to creep and dash my way back home.
But this is it: this book tells everything—
The recipes, th'experiments, the deaths.
The Apothecary's secrets all are here,
And once the Friar has them, we'll be saved.
[He suddenly becomes uneasy.]
The hour when grim night takes hold, in triumph,
Fills me with dread. The sun declines, and we
Who wander down below survive, or don't.
Phoebus, where is your car, that keeps us safe?
Why are the streets so empty? Windows dark:
No souls abroad, or so it seems...

[The PAGE appears, now a mindless revenant. BALTHASAR gasps. Another creature appears, then another...]

BALTHASAR
Oh no—

*[As one, the creatures swing their heads and see him.
This is the full horde now, and they close in.
BALTHASAR tries to escape, tries to beat them away with
the book, but there are too many. He is surrounded. He
screams as he vanishes in the horde, which carries him
off, screaming. The book remains in the middle of the
stage. After a beat, the SECOND SEARCHER runs in,
looking for the source of the screaming.]*

SECOND SEARCHER
Sister? *[She sees the book, and picks it up. She opens it.]*
        Oh, gods.

*[FRIAR LAWRENCE, ROMEO, JULIET, and
MERCUTIO enter together. The SECOND SEARCHER
looks up from the book and sees them. We hear the Horde
returning.]*

FRIAR LAWRENCE
Quick! Come with us!

*[The SECOND SEARCHER joins them and they run
offstage. Blackout.]*

INTERMISSION

ACT IV, SCENE 1
Verona: The Graveyard, midnight

[Cloaked and hooded, the FIRST SEARCHER drops a heavy body onto a heap of new-dug corpses. She removes her hood. She sings.]

[A SONG]
Death comes knocking at the door
Singing siren songs
Death comes singing songs of yore
Death comes singing songs

Death is easy, but 'tis strange
For what happens after?
If your life has been a cage
What will happen after?

Never was there life sans sorrow
To love, to lose, to love
Wake again and face the morrow
To love, to love, to love.

Wish for freedom, wish for ease
Life will take these from you
Death will offer mysteries
Death will bring you mysteries
Death will open mysteries
The offer is before you
The offer is before you
The offer

[Sometime before the end of the song, the APOTHECARY enters with a torch.]

APOTHECARY
Why do you sing to the dead?

FIRST SEARCHER
I do not know. To soothe their passing? To soothe my
own?

APOTHECARY
There is no soothing it.

FIRST SEARCHER
No?

APOTHECARY
If your hunger be for food, eat, and be full. Slake a thirst
with water. But these hungers, for other things: they can
never be sated. The void asks for more, always.

FIRST SEARCHER
I feel empty.

APOTHECARY
Let's begin.
Have you the tools and instruments we need?

FIRST SEARCHER
I do my lord.

APOTHECARY
        And do you wish to see
The fearsome rites that I perform tonight?

FIRST SEARCHER
I do my lord.

APOTHECARY
You've jettisoned your insubordination?
You vow to follow me where'er I lead?

FIRST SEARCHER
I do, my lord. I take the oath. I crave
The power and the knowledge of the dark.

APOTHECARY
And have you brought the fodder for the feast?

[The FIRST SEARCHER pulls two bound, hooded forms
from the darkness.]

FIRST SEARCHER
I have, my lord.

APOTHECARY
Are you prepared to make the sacrifice?

FIRST SEARCHER
I am, my lord.

APOTHECARY
                    Then doff thy former self
And step into the circle, acolyte.

[The FIRST SEARCHER does so.]

APOTHECARY
In this place, I am a god. Forget it not.
[He paints an evil-looking symbol on the FIRST
SEARCHER'S forehead.]
Now you belong to the dark.
You serve the spirits with both hands.

FIRST SEARCHER
I serve the spirits with both hands.

APOTHECARY
These corpses are hungry. What would you feed them?

FIRST SEARCHER
Flesh. But first a dose of the Devil's trumpet,
That ravenous their hunger never cease.

APOTHECARY
Why would you do this?

FIRST SEARCHER
I serve the spirits with both hands.

APOTHECARY
Why?

FIRST SEARCHER
I serve the spirits with both hands!

APOTHECARY
Tell them!

FIRST SEARCHER
I serve the spirits with both hands!

APOTHECARY
Then serve them. *[He shoves her onto the pile of corpses.]*
What do you have to offer to the dead?

FIRST SEARCHER
A creature who bears poison in her blood.

*[She stands, then brings one of the forms forward,
removing its hood to reveal LADY CAPULET, gagged.]*
And a dead man who was a murderer.
*[Removing the second hood to reveal TYBALT, also
gagged.]*

APOTHECARY
Why, Tybalt, King of Cats, you do me honor.
And Lady Capulet! I know your features well.

*[She utters something unintelligible behind the gag. Her
attempts to speak are indicated below by asterisks.]*

APOTHECARY
What's that? You don't know mine? Of course you don't.
And yet I know you and your family.*
Did you ask me how? Your pet ecclesiast
Was once my teacher—you know, your Friar?
I wonder, do you know much of his past?
Before he baptized your little girl
And found what he called revelation,
And changed from a man who sought to know
Into a man who sought to keep others
From knowing?* Ah, I cannot understand you.
No matter, though, I do not need your voice.
I am, however, curious. Remove
Her gag, and if she truly speaks, let's hear.

*[The FIRST SEARCHER removes LADY CAPULET's
gag. LADY CAPULET spits in the APOTHECARY's face,
and snaps at him, trying to bite him.]*

No biting, lady, sure, such coarseness is
Beneath you. Can you speak?

LADY CAPULET
                    I can curse,
And curse you I do, with all the force of hell:
May your words turn to ashes in your mouth,
Your evil plans to dust—

APOTHECARY
                    Stop up her mouth again.

[The FIRST SEARCHER replaces the gag.]

So it is true. The talking dead exist:
They'll even curse at you. I'll try a thing.
Uncover's mouth and nose.

*[The APOTHECARY takes a thimbleful of powder from
his pouch as the FIRST SEARCHER remove's TYBALT's
gag. He blows it in TYBALT's face. TYBALT blinks
against it, not subdued at all. He considers the
APOTHECARY with great compassion.]*

TYBALT
I see you. Release us. I see your pain.

APOTHECARY
You don't see me. What do you mean, you see me?

TYBALT
You need but let us go. Each choice we make
Carries its price, paid unto us or by us.

APOTHECARY
I like my choices.

TYBALT
                You will not like them
So well when you are called upon to make
A reckoning. I know this. Release us.

APOTHECARY
You shut your mouth, killer. Shut it for him!

*[The FIRST SEARCHER pushes the gag back into
TYBALT's mouth and pulls the hood back over his head.]*

APOTHECARY
This will not do. The *coup poudré* has no
Effect on him. The talkers must be killed.
All of them. You'll handle that?

FIRST SEARCHER
                Yes, my lord.

APOTHECARY
Start with these two. I need a bit of bone.
The fresh-dead make the best ingredient,
And who more fresher dead than these back-talkers?
Take them, and bring me back from each a little
Piece of skull.

FIRST SEARCHER
  I will, my lord.

[The FIRST SEARCHER leads the captives off. The APOTHECARY whispers in a low, repetitive drone as he moves to the corpses and begins marking symbols on their foreheads.]

APOTHECARY
With both hands, I serve the spirits
With both hands, I serve the spirits
Concombre zombi, concombre diable
Nuit de mort, nuit sans cesse—

[There is a violent commotion offstage, at which the APOTHECARY looks up sharply. The FIRST SEARCHER re-enters, clearly injured, carrying a single bloody scalp.]

APOTHECARY
Only one?

FIRST SEARCHER
  Tybalt escaped, my lord.

APOTHECARY
                    Did he?
Your knots, perhaps, were not tied tight enough?

[The FIRST SEARCHER is silent. The APOTHECARY takes the scalp, shaves a small chip of the bone into his mortar and grinds it.]

APOTHECARY
You are no child. Your weakness is not charming.
You've made your choice.

*[He takes a handful of powder from the mortar and
throws it on the heap of bodies. The two stand back. For
a moment, nothing. Then the dead begin to rise.]*

APOTHECARY
Rise, rise and serve me!
My revenants, my Lazarenes, my horde!
Be born again to scourge the universe.
Feed them, acolyte.

*[The FIRST SEARCHER produces a chunk of flesh and
throws it to the risen dead, who fight for it and eat it.]*

APOTHECARY
One more instruction for you, acolyte:
Your sister Searcher. I'll need you to kill her.
We cannot let a threat like her run loose.
You understand?
[He waits. Finally, The FIRST SEARCHER nods.]
Good. Now, bring them.

*[He exits. The FIRST SEARCHER waves another chunk
of flesh at the horde, who turn towards her. Wand out,
balancing terror and control like a lion tamer, she lures
them off.]*

ACT IV, SCENE 2
Verona—The Friar's cell

[JULIET, ROMEO, the FRIAR, MERCUTIO, and the
SECOND SEARCHER burst into the Friar's laboratory.
They barricade the door. JULIET takes up a position to
one side, staring fierce and fearful through the slats
hammered over the window. The SECOND SEARCHER
glares around suspiciously. MERCUTIO takes a step
toward her; she throws down the book and falls into a
fighting stance.]

FRIAR LAWRENCE
Hold! He's not your enemy.
Mercutio, stand down. Give me that book.

[JULIET picks up the book, making fraught eye contact
with the SECOND SEARCHER. She hands it to the
FRIAR and returns to her post at the window.]

SECOND SEARCHER
I know you, Friar. You're a meddler, but
Not a bad man. These monsters in your room
Attacked me this morning. But here you shield them.
Why would you do so?

FRIAR LAWRENCE
Searcher,
Your duty is an honorable one.
But you deal more in violence than in science.
These three are something never known before:
Anomalies, a mystery that faith
And nature must conspire to solve.

[*FRIAR LAWRENCE turns to the book as The SECOND SEARCHER waves off his mysticism. The atmosphere remains taut with suspicion.*]

FRIAR LAWRENCE
Where did you get this book?

SECOND SEARCHER
                    T'was on the ground.
I picked it up just as you came upon me.
Will it solve your "mystery," do you think?

ROMEO
Yes, will it tell us…what we are?
How did this happen? How are we alive?

FRIAR LAWRENCE
You're not alive, my boy, and yet not dead:
At least not as we're wont to think of it.
This thing is not unknown in history—
That by some magic, devilish or good,
The flesh reanimates, and walks the earth.
This creature *[Holding up the brain sample from earlier.]*
                    was that kind of ancient scourge:
And those who chased us here, the mindless horde—
But what I see in you, and in your love,
I've never seen, nor read nor heard of neither.
The corpse that walks, and holds its spirit too—
That death can seize the body, not the mind:
That psyche revives in the revenant—
This is a combination never known before.

ROMEO *[insistent]*
But are we damned? Are we like those outside?

FRIAR LAWRENCE
Peace, boy, keep your voice low. The horde without
Would gladly tear your throat out, dead or no.
This is what I believe:
A drug I gave Juliet, which mimics death.
You know I have some skill with medicines;
You've no idea how deep my knowledge goes.
My drug was in her body when she died.
But of itself it could not have produced
This precedentless miracle effect.

[JULIET stays pensive by the window.]

ROMEO
Juliet, didst drink some other draught that night?

JULIET
No drink. Nor no food neither.

FRIAR LAWRENCE

                                                    Are you sure?

JULIET *[fiercely]*
As sure as I sucked poison from his lips,
But could not find enough in them to die.
Remember that I stuck a dagger here, *[Indicating her
breast.]*
And died as sharp a death as could be found?

ROMEO
Hush, Julie, love, my nightingale—

JULIET
I saw my Nurse. She would have eaten me,
Had Romeo not pulled me quick away.

FRIAR LAWRENCE
You drank the same poison that killed Romeo?

JULIET
I licked the bottle and sucked at his lips,
But there was not enough to poison me.

FRIAR LAWRENCE
But you drank some?

JULIET

                         A drop or two, no more.

FRIAR
That drop was then enough. Unprecedented...
The mixture, volatile, unthought of—
In you, the birth of immortality.
You drank my drug, you drank his drug, and died.
The tincture brought you back, your self intact.
But that cannot explain--

*[Arms burst through the wooden slats of the window and
seize JULIET. She screams and struggles. The others
leap to her aid. At last, ROMEO succeeds in pulling her
free. She breaks from him, wildly:]*

JULIET
Is that all we are? Hands and teeth and hunger?
What have you made of me? I should be dead!

FRIAR
Juliet—

JULIET
I ripped the Prince's throat out with my teeth!
Who's next? Will I be hungry soon again?
Bury me deep, let me smother in earth
And never feed on flesh, or serve as food
For mindless, ravenous, devouring mouths.

ROMEO
Then bury me too, in the self-same grave!
I will not live without thee, Juliet.
Whatever life may be, I will not live
Apart from thee. Knowest thou what torture t'was
In Mantua, exiled from thou? In life, in death,
Thou art my lodestar, my anchor, my truth:
My first and final purpose is to love thee,
Juliet. Take that, and I am empty
As a shell.

SECOND SEARCHER
I'm leaving.

FRIAR LAWRENCE
                    Child, you mustn't—

SECOND SEARCHER
                                        I'm not your child.
My sister is out there, without me, fulfilling
Our sacred duty and our oath to fight
This evil scourge. I'll take your word that these
Are not a threat—but I'll not let you keep
Me from my work.

JULIET

                                     Friar, let her go.

She means to keep us safe.

MERCUTIO

                                       I will go too.

A little girl like you should have a bodyguard.

[The SECOND SEARCHER deftly disarms MERCUTIO, taking him to the ground and threatening a very delicate part of his anatomy with her wand.]

SECOND SEARCHER
A little boy like you should watch his mouth.

[FRIAR LAWRENCE turns a page in the grimoire and gasps.]

MERCUTIO
What is it, Friar?

[They all look at the book.]

SECOND SEARCHER
He's making the undead?

FRIAR LAWRENCE
He's animating corpses, and the living
Will be murdered by the dead,
Until he is the sole soul left alive.
He means to turn the world into his slaves.

JULIET
We must stop him.

SECOND SEARCHER and MERCUTIO
                          Aye, I'd say we do.

[They share a look.]

ROMEO
How?

FRIAR LAWRENCE
                          We shall have to kill him.
The revenants already in his thrall
Will fight us viciously. We'll need weapons.

*[ROMEO and MERCUTIO draw their swords. The
SECOND SEARCHER holds up her wand. JULIET...
pulls the dagger from her heart and holds it up
tentatively.]*

FRIAR LAWRENCE
Not enough.

JULIET
We have some weapons at our house. A weapons room,
actually—you know how my father is. Was?

ROMEO
We'll to the Capulet estate, to arm us there.
It isn't far.

SECOND SEARCHER
                          I have to find my sister.

ROMEO
Of course. We'll go in teams. Mercutio
Might be of some assistance to you, lady.

MERCUTIO
Two is better than one, when monsters are about.

SECOND SEARCHER
Ugh. We'll find you at the Capulets.

[She moves to leave.]

JULIET
What is your name? I should like to know it.

SECOND SEARCHER
Maeve.

JULIET
                    Thank you, Maeve.

*[After a short pause, the SECOND SEARCHER nods. She
and MERCUTIO exit.]*

FRIAR LAWRENCE
I'll fetch...supplies.
*[The FRIAR exits to his inner sanctum, leaving ROMEO
and JULIET alone.]*

ROMEO
How dost thou, Juliet?

JULIET
                              Not well, my lord.
I dreamed I was a girl in Verona.
I had a home, a nurse, a garden that I loved,
I met a boy, like me bred in Verona:
When first I heard his voice a part of me

Awaked that I had not known to be sleeping;
Hearing him, I bloomed, as he were a sun,
And I the firstling flower of the world.
But dreams are liars. Art thou Romeo?

ROMEO
Ay, lady, he.

JULIET
                 Hast any proof?
My love, my lord, my husband, and my friend
Of these five days: might you not be
A fever of the mind, a pretty madness,
A figment made of death and drug and dream?

ROMEO
I am here, with you.

JULIET
             A dream might say as much.
I feared I should go mad, i'th' tomb, if I
Awaked ere you had come. Perhaps I did,
And bashed my head in, and we are in hell.
Flung here without benefit of instruction
To push our way through bones and snapping teeth,
To bleed and fight and wander in these torments.

ROMEO
Do you love me?

JULIET
              I do. Past everything.

ROMEO
No hell could brook such love, and be a hell.
I cannot tell if this be real. Who can?
How can we ever know? Was't real, when I
First saw thee shining in thy parents' house?
Was't real when I climbed up thy orchard walls
A second time, from inside out, transformed
From doting boy into a man in love?
Or was it real when I left Tybalt dead,
Not thirty minutes married, and a killer?
Or when I told old Death he must be envious,
To keep such beauty fresh inside her tomb?
Philosophers concatenate and mull,
Let them with cobwebs dab away at truth:
I know it fresh. I know it matters not
But that I do my best with what I'm given.
And what I'm given is to love thee well:
If all the lanterns of my heart are lit
By love of thee, in loving thee I give
Light to the world. Whatever may be real,
That's what is true.

JULIET
                        Four times, we've been alone
Together. That is all. And yet it seems
A lifetime's worth of light and darkness mixed.
If we survive all this, I'd like to pass
A peaceful afternoon with thee: no ghouls,
No tombs, no future of the world at stake;
A gentle summer afternoon, a quiet breeze,
Two lovers gazing at the passing clouds.

ROMEO
We'll have that afternoon, I promise thee.

[FRIAR LAWRENCE re-enters.]

FRIAR LAWRENCE
The time grows short.

ROMEO
                              We're ready.
FRIAR LAWRENCE
                                        Haste we then.
[They move to exit, but FRIAR LAWRENCE turns back.]
I failed you. Both of you. I meant so well—
I know not if you can forgive me. I
Would ask your pardon, but it seems too small
A word. I ran away, I ran away.
[He exits. They follow him.]

ACT IV, SCENE 3
The Capulet grounds

[Enter MERCUTIO and the SECOND SEARCHER.]

MERCUTIO
What prompted you to take the Searcher's role?

SECOND SEARCHER
I had no family to marry me off
And I was good at fighting.

MERCUTIO
                         You are very
Good at fighting. Have you other talents?

SECOND SEARCHER
Yes.

MERCUTIO
Your name is Maeve?

SECOND SEARCHER
                    It is.

MERCUTIO
                    And so, at last,
Queen Mab, you come to me.

SECOND SEARCHER
                    D'you speak to me?
Or to the air?

MERCUTIO

                         To you, t' the air, to anyone
That hears—'tis not what I expected, but
'Tis good.

SECOND SEARCHER

             What's good?

MERCUTIO

                            So very many things.
Your neck, just there where it meets with your shoulder;
That fierce glint in your eye, that says I'm best
To watch my step; your arching brow, that has
Reduced me to a praiser of such parts—
The shape of your lips, and the words that fall
From them; the curve of your hips; your arms, your legs—

SECOND SEARCHER
Mercutio monster, are you tempted by my flesh?

MERCUTIO
I think you mean to trick me with this question.
Dost speak of eating? Or of other things?

SECOND SEARCHER
Say that I speak of eating.

MERCUTIO

                          Ah, again,
I fear a double meaning in your words.

SECOND SEARCHER
A monster, and afraid?

MERCUTIO

           'Tis you should be
Afraid, if I'm a monster.

SECOND SEARCHER

           Oh, I think
That I can handle you.

MERCUTIO

           I should like that.

SECOND SEARCHER
Alas, you're not the kind of man I like.
I prefer them living. In life you might
Have measured up—

MERCUTIO
           In life I was a sodding idiot.
I thought that cleverness was all that mattered—
The wild revel, the drunken brawl, the frolic:
I mocked both friend and foe for earnestness.
I never simply said a thing I felt,
But masked it all with bantering and play.
So let me say this plain—I find you fair,
And strong, and powerful and wise,
And I should like to kiss you on the mouth.
*[They kiss. Enter the FIRST SEARCHER, still holding a
chunk of flesh.]*

FIRST SEARCHER
What are you doing with that creature, sister?

SECOND SEARCHER
O! Sister! I was...what? Where have you been?

FIRST SEARCHER
Working. Do you need my help?

SECOND SEARCHER
I…no… I—we—were looking—are you hurt?

FIRST SEARCHER
A scratch. Now stand aside. I see a corpse
That wants a burial.

*[The FIRST SEARCHER offers to square off with
MERCUTIO. The SECOND SEARCHER steps between
them.]*

SECOND SEARCHER
You'll have to go through me.

MERCUTIO
                    Maeve—

[A single revenant enters behind the FIRST SEARCHER.]

SECOND SEARCHER
Sister at your back!

*[The FIRST SEARCHER spins and throws the meat to the
creature, who begins devouring it. The SEARCHERS face
each other.]*

SECOND SEARCHER
Why are you feeding that?

FIRST SEARCHER
                    Why are you kissing that?

SECOND SEARCHER
He's different. The ones who talk are different.
This you've fed, however—

*[The SECOND SEARCHER moves to kill the feeding
creature. The FIRST SEARCHER blocks her.]*

FIRST SEARCHER
I cannot let you do that. And if you
Challenge me one step further, I will kill you.

SECOND SEARCHER
What say'st thou, sister?

FIRST SEARCHER
I am not your sister. I'm stronger now.
I'm not some paper-eater, living in
The fairy tales of dusty books. I've found
A better path—a better—

*[She breaks off, unable to continue. With a hand held
forward signaling non-combativeness, the SECOND
SEARCHER steps towards her.]*

SECOND SEARCHER
Whatever you have done, it can be undone, sister—

*[The FIRST SEARCHER attacks ferociously. The
SECOND SEARCHER defends herself.]*

FIRST SEARCHER
Never call me that! A grave-robber, I,
A desecrationist, an oath-breaker!

SECOND SEARCHER
Stop this. I do not wish to harm you—

FIRST SEARCHER
                                        Ha.
I am sworn to kill you. How like you that?

SECOND SEARCHER
I like it not.

FIRST SEARCHER
                        Come on then. One of us
Must surely die tonight.

*[They fight. The FIRST SEARCHER is badly wounded
and falls.]*

FIRST SEARCHER
I did not wish to throw my life away—
I broke my vow: I sold it for a fee
That cost me more than anything I gained.
I stepped too far and in the dark no light,
No light shone forth to guide me home.
I deceived you. I failed. Forgive me, sister.

SECOND SEARCHER
Hush. All is forgiven.

APOTHECARY *[Off]*
Friar! Friar! Friar!

FIRST SEARCHER
Th'Apothecary.

Run! I think that I can stop him, but not
If you are with me. Not if he sees you
Alive, and me not killing you.

SECOND SEARCHER
                    No, sister—
My place is at your side.

FIRST SEARCHER
Get ye gone! Your place
Is fighting off this scourge, where I cannot.
Let me at least make this one last thing right.
Go. Farewell. Go.

*[The SECOND SEARCHER and MERCUTIO exit. The
APOTHECARY enters.]*

APOTHECARY
Friar!

*[Trembling, feeble, her wand up, the FIRST SEARCHER
rises.]*

FIRST SEARCHER
Turn! Turn and face me! Turn, you coward! Turn!

APOTHECARY
You disappoint me.

*[He spins around and seizes her by the neck, strangling
her until she goes limp and drops her wand. She crumples
to the ground.]*

FIRST SEARCHER
Oh, help—*[she dies]*

APOTHECARY
That's how a girl dies—with a little sob.
Never take a student. They are never,
Never you, no matter how you hope.
Send me no more girls! I'll have a friar
To my sword! Where are you, brother Lawrence?

[FRIAR LAWRENCE appears on the balcony, above.]

FRIAR LAWRENCE
Here, brother James.

APOTHECARY
I could just stand here, gazing up at you,
For all my days and nights to come, old friend,
If only I had not so very much
Murdering to do.

FRIAR LAWRENCE
Shall I hear more, or shall I speak at this?

APOTHECARY
O hear more, do, I love to speak my thoughts
And all this time I've had no audience!

[FRIAR LAWRENCE descends from the Balcony.]

FRIAR LAWRENCE
What will you say? I've seen your gramarye.
Will you vaunt the ways you've twisted Nature?

Brag of those you've slaughtered, the death you've
wrought?
Your work is evil, James! You mar the world.
What might be good is poison in your hands.
No more.

APOTHECARY
          O please you, just a wee bit more.

*[The APOTHECARY lunges at FRIAR LAWRENCE and
they fight. The APOTHECARY gains the upper hand and
attacks ferociously, unleashing all of his pent up rage on
his former master.]*

APOTHECARY
You never trusted me. You held me back,
You checked my inborn skill at every turn!
You taunted me with platitudes, scolded me
For seeking greater knowledge. You drove me out!

[TYBALT enters.]

FRIAR LAWRENCE
Tybalt—my son— help—

*[TYBALT hesitates. The APOTHECARY has his hands
around FRIAR LAWRENCE'S neck. The FRIAR gasps:]*

FRIAR LAWRENCE
James...why?

APOTHECARY
Oh yes, the why! The sacred, dreadful why!

[TYBALT stabs the APOTHECARY.]

TYBALT
Forgive me.
We are our choices, and we pay their price.

*[The APOTHECARY sputters, unintelligible, dying,
scrabbling for his pouch. FRIAR LAWRENCE kicks it out
of reach.]*

FRIAR LAWRENCE
A villain is a villain is a villain.
James. I may understand, but not excuse:
Unless you should repent... *[he waits. Nothing.]*
D'you think your early sorrows will excuse you?
Your precious human fallibility?
You made your choices, ever for the worst,
And now your life snuffs out, and none
Shall mourn your death. Though I shall grieve a bit,
For what thou mightst have been. Thou wast so angry
As a boy, but I hoped kindness would
Awake a kinder self. I see thee now,
A bloody ragged man, and wonder if
By word or deed I could have changed thy course.

*[The APOTHECARY dies. FRIAR LAWRENCE sags.
ROMEO AND JULIET run in, armed with weapons from
the armory. A beat. FRIAR LAWRENCE heaves a heavy
sigh, and turns to them. As he does so, the FIRST
SEARCHER's revenant reappears and bites the FRIAR.
He exclaims and collapses, clutching the wound. JULIET
and ROMEO face off with the creature. A fight. JULIET
kills it, brutally. FRIAR LAWRENCE is on the ground,
moaning. They run to him.]*

ROMEO
How long before you turn?

FRIAR
                                        A minute...two...

JULIET
How can we save you? There must be a way.

FRIAR
I know not, Juliet, I know not how—
'Tis close—the answer—

*[He gestures as though the answer is orbiting, hovering
just outside his brain. He is failing. His fingers touch his
lips, then JULIET's face, in a gesture that could be
farewell or something else. He dies.]*

JULIET
Father Lawrence!

ROMEO
Tybalt, get away from him. Juliet.
Mercutio attacked you, then he bit you,
Then he changed. He was mindless, like them,
But then he changed. 'Tis you. 'Tis you, my love:
You are the cure! Give me your arm—

*[He takes her arm and pulls out a knife. The FRIAR is
stirring.]*

JULIET
What dost thou Romeo?

[He slices her arm. Blood wells up, red and fresh. The FRIAR convulses. Realization dawns on JULIET.]

JULIET

My blood?

[He nods. The FRIAR contorts himself upright. JULIET kisses ROMEO, hard. She looks at the Friar, then her bleeding arm, then back to ROMEO. He nods.]

ROMEO
In his mouth.

[She turns. The FRIAR, fully changed, lets out a terrifying sound and charges. She meets him, shoving her arm into his open mouth. They grapple, the force of their collision knocking them to the ground, the FRIAR on top of JULIET. They go still. A pause.]

JULIET *[weakly]*
Romeo? Help.

[ROMEO lunges to her, with TYBALT's help lifting the FRIAR's body and helping her up.]

TYBALT
Cousin—

JULIET

Cousin.

[They embrace. As they do so, the FRIAR sneezes.]

TYBALT *[instinctively]*
Bless you.

FRIAR
Thank you.

*[ROMEO, JULIET, and TYBALT throw their arms around
the FRIAR as MERCUTIO and the SECOND SEARCHER
come smashing into the locked garden gate, breathless,
pursued by the horde.]*

SECOND SEARCHER
Unbar the gate and let us in! Quickly!

*[ROMEO rushes to do so. The SECOND SEARCHER and
MERCUTIO slam the gate shut, locking it just as the
horde arrives. It is a terrifying spectacle.]*

MERCUTIO
They're everywhere. The whole city is turned.

JULIET
Father. My blood cured you.
It cured Mercutio. Could it cure them?

FRIAR LAWRENCE
Ye gods, my daughter, it is possible!
Tybalt, quick—fetch the garden pump to me.
I think *[reaching into his satchel]* —I have it!
*[He produces a length of tubing and improvises a
connection from JULIET to the pump to the hose. The
horde is shaking the gate, on the verge of breaking in.]*

FRIAR LAWRENCE
My child, art thou prepared?

ROMEO
Friar—wait, this is not safe—

FRIAR LAWRENCE
It is our only hope for safety!

ROMEO

                                  No!

JULIET
My love, I must. Hold me tight.

ROMEO

                    And never let you go.

JULIET
I'm ready, Friar!

[FRIAR LAWRENCE starts the pouring of Juliet's blood into the pump and lifts the hose.]

FRIAR LAWRENCE
Open the gates!

[MERCUTIO and the SECOND SEARCHER open the gates. The Horde pours in. FRIAR LAWRENCE unleashes a massive spray of blood onto them. All is confusion and terror…then, the creatures collapse. Everyone is covered in blood. ROMEO holds the weakened JULIET in his arms. MERCUTIO and the

SECOND SEARCHER stand close to each other, panting with exertion. FRIAR LAWRENCE drops the hose connected to JULIET's veins. They stare at the heap of bodies, trapped in suspense, waiting to see the outcome of their dousing in JULIET's blood. One of the corpses shifts. Everyone tenses, prepared for the worst. It is BALTHASAR. He sits up. Shakes his head. Struggles to get to his feet. He gets his balance, looks around. Looks at his hands. Feels his head, his face, his chest, then lets out a huge whoop.]

BALTHASAR
WooHOOOOOOOOOO!

ROMEO
Balthasar?

BALTHASAR
You've done it, man, you've done it! There's a cure!
I'm just like you—Myself again! Alive!
Well, not alive…but now I'll never die!

FRIAR
Balthasar—

BALTHASAR
            I want to eat some flesh!
Consensually, of course.
[A cute blood-drenched girl is re-animating out of the heap.]   Rosaline!
[He swings her into a deep dip and plants a big kiss on her lips.]
I always wanted to do that.

ROSALINE

                            Me too!
You want to go t' th' butchershop with me?

BALTHASAR
I do. Adieu, my lords! The lady craves fresh meat.

[BALTHASAR and ROSALINE exit. The others come to their feet, discovering the higher consciousness of their new existence. The SECOND SEARCHER reaches into her bag and produces two crowns, one of which we last saw being fought over by Lords Capulet and Montague.]

SECOND SEARCHER
I have been carrying this pair of crowns
Whose former heads are short of bodies, now
That they've been hewn off at the neck. Friar,
I think we two are all that's left of all
The clergy and municipality…
What shall we do with these?

FRIAR LAWRENCE

                            Two fitting heads
To wear two fitted crowns. The world is new,
And leadership should match its citizens.
Dear Romeo, and Juliet, I ask of you:
Will you take up the scepter of the realm?

JULIET *[weakly]*
If thou wilt be my king, I'll be thy queen.

ROMEO
My queen, my saint, my goddess, and my love,
Forevermore.

[ROMEO kisses her. Everyone sighs appreciatively.
ROMEO and JULIET stand next to each other, ready to
be crowned.]

SECOND SEARCHER
As sole survivor of our government,
It falls on me to crown our new regent.
Kneel Romeo, and rise an emperor.
[ROMEO kneels, is crowned.]
Kneel, Juliet, and rise our empress.
[JULIET kneels, is crowned. They take hands and stand
together.]

MERCUTIO
Everyone is dead! Long live Romeo and Juliet!

ALL
Long live Romeo and Juliet!

[Cheers and kissing. ROMEO and JULIET, MERCUTIO
and SECOND SEARCHER, TYBALT finds Paris' PAGE
in the revived horde and lays a big kiss on him. Perhaps
the NURSE kisses the FRIAR. Suddenly, JULIET
swoons.]

ROMEO
My queen! O Friar, she lost too much blood!

[The FRIAR rushes to her side.]

ROMEO
Juliet! *[despairing, shaking her]* My love, stay with me!

FRIAR LAWRENCE
Hush, my lord.

[All are still, staring at the still form of JULIET. She stirs. Before they have time to be relieved, she struggles up violently and moves into a central space, holding her arms out to keep everyone away from her. After a moment, her body jerks and she looks confusedly towards her stomach. Another moment... she feels something again and gently places her hands on her midsection. A look of joy dawns on her face.]

JULIET
O, Romeo.

[Romeo places his hand on her stomach too. They look at each other, then out to the audience.]

BLACKOUT
END OF PLAY.

NOTES ON PRODUCTION

The parents of *R & J & Z* are Shakespeare on one side and modern horror films on the other. The play lives in what historian Tzvetan Todorov calls the "Fantastic Marvelous." The events that occur, though "supernatural" or fantastic, are actually happening. Therefore the laws of reality must be changed to explain the events. As with supernatural tales from *Macbeth* to *World War Z, R & J & Z* is best served by an approach in which these events are truly happening, in the world where Romeo and Juliet live—and die, and live again.

Supernatural themes notwithstanding, *R & J & Z* is grounded in historical fact. *Romeo & Juliet* was written while London's theatres were closed due to plague, and Shakespeare's text is full of gruesome allusions to death, disease, and gore. Of remarkable note are the Searchers of the Town, mentioned by Shakespeare, who become central characters in *R & J & Z*. In an era when women rarely worked outside the home, this official job was held by two adult women whose duty it was to examine all dead bodies for signs of plague. The suggestion that they also belonged to a secret order is, as far as can be known, an invention of the playwright.

—Melody Bates

NOTES

NOTES

www.ingramcontent.com/pod-product-compliance
Lightning Source LLC
LaVergne TN
LVHW051647080426
835511LV00016B/2540